STRONG WINDS & CRASHING WAVES

Meeting Jesus in the Memories of Traumatic Events

STRONG WINDS & CRASHING WAVES

Meeting Jesus in the Memories of Traumatic Events

Terry Wardle

LEAFWOOD
P U B L I S H E R S
Abilene, TX

Strong Winds and Crashing Waves

Meeting Jesus in the Memories of Traumatic Events

LEAFWOOD
PUBLISHERS

Copyright 2007 by Terry Wardle

ISBN 0-89112-512-4

Printed in the United States of America

Cover design by Rick Gibson

For information contact:
Leafwood Publishers, Abilene, Texas
1-877-816-4455 toll free
www.leafwoodpublishers.com

07 08 09 10 11 12 / 7 6 5 4 3 2 1

182721281

To
Anne Halley
For all the wounded people
you have placed in
the arms of Jesus.

CONTENTS

ACKNOWLEDGEMENTS

The journey of life is never successfully navigated alone. It takes a community of fellow travelers committed to helping each other move forward toward the destination set out before them by the Lord. And most certainly one activity that clearly illustrates this is writing a book. While there may be one person named as author, many other people who make vital contributions to the final product deserve special thanks and recognition.

My wife Cheryl continues to be a vital source of support and encouragement, for which I am eternally grateful. Special thanks goes to my children, Aaron, Cara, and Emily, my daughter-in-law Destry and son-in-law Brad, for always extending love regardless of how preoccupied I become when writing. And of course, deepest thanks goes to my three grandchildren, Grace, Allison, and Kayla, who have captured my heart and provided wonderful, life-filling breaks every time they came looking for Papa.

I am indebted to several friends and colleagues who helped refine my thoughts and in several cases read and re-read the various drafts of this book. Thanks to Dr. Doug Little, my dear friend, for constant encouragement, great wisdom, and invaluable suggestions that improved this book significantly; to Vicki Didato and Dr. Donna Thomas for reading the manuscript and contributing important ideas to better the work; to Sara Herring for spending vacation time at the beach reading and editing my writing; and to Dr. Anne Halley, whose contributions to this book and my life are inestimable.

I also want to say a special word of thanks to my colleagues, Lori Byron and Lynne Lawson, who worked tirelessly to keep programs under my supervision operating with excellence during my absence. You are both wonderful co-workers and valued friends. And finally, thanks to the faculty, administration, and trustees of Ashland Theological Seminary for providing a study leave that gave me space to write this book.

Terry Wardle

INTRODUCTION

This book is written to help two groups of people: those who struggle with the effects of traumatic wounding, and those who serve as their counselors, spiritual directors, pastors, and caregivers. It is my desire and prayer that, by being honest about my own journey through emotional upheaval and deep healing, I can offer hope to those who walk that same path. I know how frightening and lonely the battle can be. Many times I felt that no one really understood what I was going through. That made the journey all the more frustrating and difficult. If you are struggling with the effects of traumatic wounding, I hope you will find in these pages the story of a fellow pilgrim. I also pray that the specific insights I provide will serve you on the path to deep healing and help you connect with the One who has the strength to carry you through—Jesus.

This book is also written for caregivers. There are important resources, secular and Christian, that provide invaluable guidance about traumatic woundings and resulting disorders. I have been helped immensely by reading many such volumes. Their insights have contributed to my own journey as well as the help I provide to others. The uniqueness, if any, of this book is its point of view. I am writing about the effects of traumatic woundings by looking from the inside out, sharing honestly about the struggle and frustrations that accompany the journey toward healing and transformation. I do not write as a dispassionate observer providing an objective perspective on the topic. I am subjectively connected to the topic and deeply engaged emotionally.

The insights I provide here on the topic of traumatic wounding did not come to me on the mountain top of scholarly reflection and pursuit. For whatever reason, the most significant changes that have occurred in my life and in my relationship with Christ have been forged in difficulty and trial. I learn many of life's most important lessons while in the ditch. My relationship with Jesus and the pursuit of intimacy with him were actually greatly enhanced during a long season of depression. And my heartfelt concern for wounded people is in part a result of a season of my own deep brokenness. I now have far more grace for the weak and struggling because I so desperately needed grace when I walked through a time of darkness. So what I have learned about traumatic wounding and emotional healing has come in large part from my own desperate journey.

In some ways I am the poster child for "growth through falling apart." Of course that is the same for most people. We learn and grow through the trials and difficulties of life. Ronald Rolheiser wrote about an opportunity he had, as a young psychology student, to attend a lecture by Polish psychologist Casmir Dobrowski. His topic was "positive disintegration." The theory was that most people grow as a result of falling apart. Rolheiser questioned him, suggesting that surely a person can grow through success. Dabrowski responded:

> Theoretically, yes, we can grow through our successes, just as easily as we can through our failures. But I can say this; through more than forty years of psychiatric practice I have rarely seen it. Almost always deep growth takes place through the opposite— our deaths, our losses, our dark nights of the soul.[1]

This resonates with the words Jesus spoke to Paul and recorded in 2 Corinthians about grace flowing through weakness (12:9). It is when we are most in need that the strength of Christ is present to change us.

It is important for you to know that this book is not written by a clinician, nor does it come from that perspective. The thoughts I share are consistent with what many Christian counselors and psychologists hold. But I am looking at this topic from a perspective that is more spiritually driven. I have been a pastor and seminary professor for many years now, and it is that which most shapes my understanding of the healing process.

I am convinced of the power of God's healing love. God and God alone brings deep change to a person's life. I have not only seen him do that in the lives of many broken people, I have experienced the transforming power of that touch myself. The Father does more than simply help people cope with the problems they carry. The Lord meets them in those problems, draws them close in his arms of love, strengthens them by the power of the Holy Spirit, and ultimately changes their lives forever.

For almost fifteen years I have taught, counseled, and written about the healing of memories. For most of that time I referred to that process as *inner healing prayer*. However, for the past few years I have stopped using that phrase, calling the process *formational prayer* instead. I made that change for several reasons. First, I found that the term "inner healing" immediately caused some people to be closed to the process. It is used broadly today and in some cases is attached to practices that are both unbiblical and unhelpful. I have at times had people oppose what I was teaching before they even understood the model I was proposing. They were closed simply because of the baggage that comes with the term "inner healing." That is unfortunate because I do believe the phrase "inner healing" describes what takes place deep within a wounded person when Jesus touches him or her. All my other books on the topic employ that phrase. Nevertheless, to help people keep an open mind about the process, I have made the change to *formational prayer*.

There have also been important positive reasons for referring to the process as *formational prayer*. God has made it clear that he wants to transform us into the image of Jesus Christ. And it is through that transformation that we experience ever increasing degrees of freedom, accomplished through the power of the Holy Spirit (Romans 8:29, and 2 Corinthians 3:17 and 18). Inviting the Lord, through guided prayer, into the places of deep traumatic wounding and debilitating memories is actually part of that process. It is a way that the Spirit sanctifies the believer's life. Through prayer Jesus is actually forming the wounded person into his likeness. He is entering the darkness of the past to bring healing light to broken places so that the person can walk in the freedom he provided on Calvary.

I also refer to the process as *formational prayer* because I want it to be linked to the literature and practice of spiritual formation. I have great appreciation for the insights gained through the social and behavioral sciences. And I would not be where I am today, either personally or professionally, were it not for some of their help. However, I am concerned that there are those, even in the Christian community, who believe that helping people with deep emotional problems is the exclusive business of the counseling and psychological community. They are certainly part of the solution. An important part. And there are levels of brokenness that demand great expertise and sensitivity. But caring for the wounded and broken is also the call of the church, and the literature and disciplines of Christian spiritual formation have a contribution to make to the process.

Many people have been helped through the dark night of the soul by looking to the literature and disciplines of spiritual formation. For centuries the fathers and mothers of the church have provided rich and invaluable guidance on traversing the treacherous valleys of life. I discovered that literature during the time of my deepest distress. And I found principles there that helped me experience Jesus in ways I had never before considered. And their insights invariably included a great emphasis on the importance of meeting the Lord in prayer during times of brokenness and struggle.

Simply stated, *formational prayer* is the term I use to describe the process of helping a broken person meet Christ in the pain-filled wounds of the past in order to set them free from the lies, distress, and dysfunctional behaviors that are keeping them in bondage. Formational prayer is a model of care that opens the way for the Holy Spirit to move through a gifted caregiver, touching a broken person where he or she most needs release and transformation. Whenever the term *formational prayer* is used in this book, it is referring to that meaning and process.

Chapter One focuses upon the difficult journey victims of traumatic wounding face and the foundational concepts of wounded healer, transformation, grace, and the love of God. Chapter Two shares the story of my own struggle, providing a "view from the inside." I hope that it will help both fellow pilgrims and those who are committed to walking with them toward freedom. Chapter Three presents a basic typology of traumatic wounding and looks at the effects such events have on people's lives and relationships. Chapters Four and Five detail a list of twelve resources I believe essential to moving successfully through the process of healing. Chapter Six discusses a specific strategy for encountering Christ through the process of formational prayer. Finally, Chapter Seven closes the book with a discussion of the ministry of the Holy Spirit and how he works to empower the broken for continued healing and ongoing freedom.

Terry Wardle
Ashland, Ohio
June, 2006

Chapter One

BROKEN REED, SMOLDERING WICK

Henri Nouwen once wrote that there will be times in life when a person will be taken on a journey not of their own choosing. Those who have struggled with the difficult and at times debilitating affects of emotional wounding and resulting psychological disorders know just how true that statement is. No one would ever choose to walk through life on a path that is as difficult and in many ways as nightmarish as that taken by the victims of traumatic events. It seems like a never ending journey that is at times tolerable, but most often deeply distressing. It is a treacherous and lonely path that exacts a costly toll, paid for relationally, physically, emotionally, and spiritually.

Shame and the frustration that comes when friends and families do not understand lead many to withdraw and isolate, making things worse. I remember being introduced to a leading political figure in

Ohio one day soon after joining the faculty of Ashland Theological Seminary. He asked what I did. I told him that I taught at a seminary and worked with people who were having difficulty in life because of traumatic wounds of the past. His answer was harsh, but fairly typical for people in our performance based society. He said, "In my opinion, all these people need is a swift kick in the ass and told to get up and get moving."

He could tell by my body language that I did not appreciate what he said, and after a moment when I simply stared at him, he asked, "So how did these people you help get so messed up anyway?" I admit that my response was not gracious, but I was angry and not in the mood to play politics with the issue. I said, "They got so messed up as you put it because they were raised around people who did not care about their hurts and who simply kicked them in the ass and told them to get moving." He knew by my words and the tone of my delivery that on this issue I was not going to play nice. He stood looking at me for a moment and then said, "Well, I guess I do not really understand." I simply replied, "No sir, you don't understand, and that's too bad."

The energy behind my response did not come simply because I have been touched by the wonderful people I have met over the years who struggle with emotional problems. I was speaking out of my own frustration with that type of insensitivity, because I have personally battled with the affects of traumatic wounding for years. I have been on a difficult journey for a long time. In my case, some of the most traumatic events occurred while I was an infant and small child. As a result my earliest memories are of long sleepless nights awake in bed facing the darkest emptiness imaginable. As a child I felt tremendous insecurity, which was frustrating to my parents. During adolescence I learned to kill the pain of unrelenting anxiety through a variety of coping strategies, which in the long run did far more damage than good. I became a Christian in my early twenties and tried to work hard for Christ as an antidote to the ongoing internal storm. But no matter what I did, the anxiety was never far away. By my late thirties everything came crashing in, and the unaddressed and unprocessed events of my past brought a tremendous emotional storm that was debilitating, requiring hospitalization.

I have received great help over the past fourteen years, and have experienced Jesus in many unexpected ways. He has consistently met me in the places of darkness and pain lodged deep within my soul. There, where I never anticipated finding him, Jesus extended grace-filled love and healing to me. Through Christ I have been able to move out of the virtual bondage of a full blown anxiety disorder to a productive life, even contributing to the healing of others. Many times I encountered the Lord through formational prayer, which enabled me to face unresolved issues that were crippling my life. And, because of his compassionate touch, I have been empowered to move forward with joy and tremendous freedom.

Yet, the journey toward healing continues and it is seldom easy. I must admit that fear and anxiety are often in my side-view mirror. On most days I am able to function well. I ask the Holy Spirit to help me through the day and he gives me the strength to move forward with confidence. But if triggered, I can suddenly regress into levels of terror and panic that can distort my perspective and cause me to isolate in shame and fear. Simply stated, I have struggled with post traumatic stress disorder for a long time, and it has been a tough journey. Jesus faithfully meets me there, helping me find release from the unprocessed pain of deep wounding. He has empowered me to keep moving forward toward the abundant life he promised. But the journey continues, and while I am healing, I am not yet healed.

There are four concepts that are fundamental to this book and the process of deep inner healing. I address each of them in the following section in order to lay a foundation for what comes in the remaining chapters. The topics are 1) the wounded healer, 2) transformation, 3) grace, and 4) the love of God. They are presented briefly, yet are of critical importance to the discussion. I have attempted to present each in a way that brings both basic understanding of the topic and its relevance to the journey with Jesus into memories of traumatic events.

The Wounded Healer

Fourteen years ago I had a visit from a ministerial colleague who shared some advice that I have never forgotten. I had just been released from the hospital where I was being treated for depression and severe anxiety. I am sure that he came to see me out of genuine affection and concern for me and for my ministry. During his visit he strongly advised me never to tell people that I had been in the hospital for depression and fear. He said that if I did I would sacrifice credibility with people and ultimately lose my ministry.

Obviously I did not follow his guidance, choosing over the years to be vulnerable about my own journey through depression and pain. And, despite his concerns, doing so has not summarily disqualified me in the eyes of everyone. In many ways it has opened the way for me to minister to many wonderful people who have struggled with emotional disorders similar to mine. It has turned out just as Jesus said it would (2 Corinthians 12:9). Out of my weakness, the strength of Jesus has poured forth to touch many broken men, women, and children. The places of pain and brokenness have become vehicles of his healing presence. It has been all about his grace, not my strength. That is the upside down nature of the Kingdom of God, which often baffles people, even Christ's own followers.

In our society, strength and objectivity are greatly valued, particularly in professions like pastoral care and counseling. The reigning philosophy is that caregivers should seek to "know without being known." I have many friends in ministry who would never admit personal struggles, fearing that people would not take them seriously as servants of the Lord. They have been taught to maintain professional objectivity at all times, keeping their weaknesses well out of sight. While there may be some merit in such an approach to care, it is not the only acceptable way to help broken people. In fact, when considering the cross of Christ, it would seem that there is great room for vulnerability and weakness.

Jesus defeated the forces of darkness, not by a display of nuclear level force, but by hanging helplessly at Calvary. There, as Paul wrote, Jesus disarmed all powers and authorities (Colossians 2:15). Faced with military, economic, religious, political, and spiritual opposition, Jesus took the stance of weakness, going to Calvary like a lamb being led to the slaughter. It appeared as though darkness was more powerful than light and that good was swept away by evil. However, in some mysterious way, by saying yes to the crucifixion Jesus unleashed God's awesome power to save a lost and broken world. The wounds that were meant to defeat Jesus became channels of healing and are precious in the sight of the redeemed. Christians across the globe celebrate the Eucharist as a constant reminder of the shedding of Christ's blood and the breaking of his body. From those wounds flow healing life to all who believe.

Henri Nouwen referred to Jesus as the Wounded Healer, and challenged Christians to become like him for the lost and broken of the world. Nouwen's basic thesis was that people must be attentive to their own wounds, bringing them to Jesus for healing. But as they do, believers should be open to helping others who are similarly struggling in life. As they experience Christ in the place of brokenness, Christians are to turn and use that encounter as the context for helping others. In his book, *The Wounded Healer*, Nouwen told the following story.

Rabbi Yoshua ben Levi came upon Elijah the prophet while he was standing at the entrance of Rabbi Simeron ben Yohai's cave . . . He asked Elijah, "When will the Messiah come?" Elijah replied, "Go and ask him yourself." "Where is He?" "Sitting at the gates of the city." "How shall I know him?" "He is sitting among the poor covered with wounds...he unbinds one at a time and binds it up again, saying to himself, perhaps I shall be needed; if so I must always be ready so as not to delay for a moment."[2]

Nouwen goes on to comment.

The Messiah, the story tells us, is sitting among the poor, binding his wounds one at a time, waiting for the moment when he will be needed. So it is too with the minister . . . he must bind his own wounds carefully in anticipation of the moment when he is needed. He is called to be the wounded healer, the one who must look after his own wounds, but at the same time be prepared to heal the wounds of others.[3]

Nouwen challenged Christians to minister with great sympathy for the human condition. This comes by facing one's woundedness and surrendering it to Christ's healing touch. That weakness then becomes the strength of Jesus, and the experience of pain the common ground that binds people to the lost and broken. This is what the Lord did when, broken at Calvary, he offered people healing and freedom through his wounds. Now, as wounded healers, people are to openly admit woundedness while at the same time extend hope and healing to others.

I have been deeply touched by the ministry of wounded healers who have been open about their own struggles while pointing others to the healing presence of Christ. People like Larry Crabb, Henri Nouwen, Brennan Manning, Andy Comisky, Gerald May, Robert McGee, Joni Earickson-Tada, Charles Colson, and Gordon MacDonald have profoundly impacted my life and my approach to ministry. They have learned that the object of great pain can become the source of blessing when surrendered to Christ. For them, pretending or putting on a pretty face is of no value whatsoever. What counts is the strength of Christ Jesus, made perfect in the weakness of frail, suffering human beings who find healing in his wounds. In turn, these men and women humbly offer their own wounds as a context for Christ's ministry to other broken men and women. When treated like this, personal wounds do not offend; they attract people to the Lord Jesus.

I share all this for one important reason. I am making a conscious choice to approach this book from the model of the wounded healer. I do not write as one who has arrived. I am clearly on a journey with Jesus and I have much terrain yet to traverse. For some, that confession may make it difficult to seriously consider what I am proposing. There may even be those who will find my openness as reason to dismiss my insights on the treatment of PTSD and other emotional problems. I understand that and am willing to face such reactions—and any other risks of personal vulnerability. It is worth it to me because I know many people will identify with what I share and find encouragement to look to Jesus for healing and freedom much as I am doing.

I am consciously stepping away from the "know but not be known" paradigm of professional objectivity. I am instead embracing a "be known so that others might know and experience Jesus" approach to writing. I am choosing to be open about my weakness because it gives me opportunity, like Paul, to boast all the more in Christ (2 Corinthians 12: 9 and 10). Ultimately this entire book is about Jesus and his willingness to meet people in weakness and bring his healing strength to their lives. I am not at all concerned that people end up seeing me as struggling and weak. I am in many ways weak and I do in fact struggle along the way. But I do want readers to know that Jesus is strong, full of grace, and ready to touch them in the places of deep wounding and pain. He wants to do far more than help people with their problems. Jesus wants to transform them into his own likeness and bring ever increasing levels of freedom to their lives.

Transformation

Frankly, when locked in a PTSD episode, my first thought is not, "Maybe Jesus will use this to transform me in some way." I am far more concerned that I get relief from the emotional pain I am experiencing and I want to find some solid ground to stand on again. When the waves are crushing against me and the winds too strong for me to stand, I want relief, not deep personal change. Emotionally, I am simply trying to survive and have little thought or interest in some theological concept like transformation. I simply want the pain to go away.

But broken people, like me, need to realize that transformation is at the heart of deep personal healing. It is a work of the Holy Spirit that is accomplished as individuals allow God to bring deep change to the way they think, feel, and act in life. Given how distorted thoughts, feelings, and actions can be for wounded people, it is change that is both needed and welcome. Essentially, the Holy Spirit works to cause believers to be more and more like Jesus. He does that so that they can have increasing intimacy with the Father, like Jesus did, and have his strength of character when facing life's trials and storms. This transformation is a great gift from God. Instead of simply relieving the strong winds and crushing waves that come with life, as I often ask him to do, God works to transform people to move through storms like Christ. Transformation is an ongoing process that instills the nature of Christ and the virtues of his character within believing people.

When asked why Christ died on Calvary, most Christians will say that his death was payment for sin which provides forgiveness to the penitent believer and freedom from eternal damnation. That answer is certainly not wrong, but it is a limited perspective on the redemptive work of Christ. Jesus shed his blood to accomplish far more than just "white out" for sins listed on God's record book. Jesus gave his life so that people could be changed at the deepest level of their being. Paul spoke of this in 2 Corinthians:

> Now the Lord is the Spirit, and where the Spirit of the Lord is, there is freedom. And we, who with unveiled faces all reflect the Lord's glory, are being transformed into his likeness with ever increasing glory, which comes from the Lord, who is the Spirit. (2 Corinthians 3:17, 18)

Jesus does not simply wipe away past mistakes, as important as that is. He has made it possible for people to undergo deep personal transformation. Those who receive Christ as Lord and Savior are indwelt by the Holy Spirit. And, as this passage suggests, the Spirit moves to change them every day in countless ways.

What does that have to do with the topic of emotional trauma and the healing of memories? The process of healing is part of the transformation mentioned in 2 Corinthians 3. Instead of being locked in the bondage of fear, anxiety, anger, and depression, Christians can increasingly experience the peace, joy, patience, and strength of Christ. It happens as people invite the Lord into the places of pain and darkness that compromise their well being. It is not an easy process nor does it happen quickly. Admittedly there are times when I wonder if I am changing at all. Yet each time a broken person allows the Holy Spirit to work within him or her, transformation is taking place.

Last spring I went into our yard to clear the flowerbeds of leaves. The winter was long, cold, and very wet. Many leaves had accumulated in the flower beds and were lying on the ground, wet and heavy. But as I began to rake them away I was taken aback by what I saw. There, deep beneath the old, wet, smothering leaves, were small, bent over, yellowish green shoots trying to live. The winter debris had been holding them down and restricting their growth. But they were there trying to live just the same. I pulled away the leaves, and the shoots were exposed to the warm sun, the air, and the spring rains. Within days those shoots turned the brightest green, straightened to the sun and began to grow. Today those shoots, long buried by the winter, are flowers in all their glory, displaying the beauty of God's good creation.

That is what the process of deep healing and transformation is all about. The Holy Spirit, through deep healing prayer, works with broken people to clear out all the accumulated debris that is restricting freedom and growth. He helps them release the pent up emotions that remain from unprocessed traumatic events. The Spirit reveals destructive lies and helps willing people replace them with God's truth. He enables people to experience Jesus in the painful memory in a way that brings healing. Jesus makes it possible for believers to change what they believe about themselves.

The Spirit also brings healing to people's minds, freeing their brains to work as God created. And he equips the wounded to walk in freedom, even using them as instruments of healing in the lives of others. And through it all, Christians are able to experience a new and deeper relationship with Christ, which is by far the greatest benefit of all. It will be as Paul said in 2 Corinthians 5, "Therefore, if anyone is in Christ, he is a new creation; the old has gone, the new has come! All this is from God, who reconciled us to himself through Christ and gave us the ministry of reconciliation" (5:17, 18). This passage affirms the promise of transformation, which should be an anchor of hope for all those who, like me, walk along that difficult journey that was not of their own choosing.

I know that it is a tough path, and that there are days when people wonder if it will ever be easier, let alone come to an end. When the storm of emotional disorder rages, most people do little more than hope for survival. The concept of actual change is hardly considered. But the promise of scripture is true, for I have experienced that healing touch of Jesus many times. Once again, I am not saying that the process of transformation is easy or that it happens quickly. But just as the scripture says, old things do pass away and new life does come. Transformation is often experienced as a small shoot growing in the midst of heavy leaves and debris. But it does happen and with the Spirit's help it will grow.

And what is more amazing is that this promised freedom is available to every broken person as a gift of God, made possible through the sacrifice of Christ. It comes to people who are willing to invite Christ into the broken places and there experience his transforming presence. Transformation does not come by striving, performing, or working hard at self-improvement. It comes to wounded people who ask the Lord not to simply help them out of storms, but to change them in the very midst of them. And it comes to the wounded by the grace of God.

Grace

The notion of grace is not easily understood or embraced by most people. That certainly has been true for me. The idea of unmerited favor does not easily register, particularly given the performance driven and punishment inducing environment of American culture. Years ago, a famous actor named John Houseman did a series of commercials for the investment firm of Smith Barney. In each he would eventually growl, "Smith Barney makes money the old fashioned way. They earn it!"

That was the philosophy of life I was taught. I get what I earn. And that was not simply the way to get money. It was the formula for all of life. If I wanted to get ahead, I must earn it. If I wanted acceptance, it would come by doing those things that bring acceptance. Even love was linked to performance. Do things right and well, there is love to be experienced. Falter or fail, and there too I could expect to get what I earned, which would most likely be rejection or punishment. Earning it, regardless of what it was, was the way of life.

Certainly education was built on that model, particularly when I was in school during the fifties and sixties. A student was rewarded according to performance. Those who earned A's were the number ones, praised by the teacher and given special stars and stickers and seats in the front. The slow, or slothful, or misbehaving, as defined back then, were shamed and shunned accordingly. By that method, it was believed that students would, by either positive or negative reinforcement, be motivated to do their best.

My experience with athletics was little different. I loved basketball and as an eighth grade student made the junior high team. Even at that level, the coach's desire to win was fanatical. Defeating the opposing teams was the only acceptable outcome for him, so he drove players to do their best, not for joy of the game, but to put a win in the column. He had recently left the Marine Corps, and brought that drill sergeant mentality to practice and the game.

For two years Coach Collins sought to motivate us to excel by calling us names, threatening physical harm, and displaying outbursts of anger that were way out of line. But his tactics did not work. Most all of us were scared to death, which only increased his ridicule and threats of being benched or worse, thrown off the team. And he made one thing consistently clear: we lost games because we were losers. We got what we deserved. By the tenth grade I quit basketball, never to play it again as an organized sport. I simply tired of trying to earn the approval of my disapproving coach.

Many people try to take that "earn it" philosophy into their relationship with God. While most Christians have heard and possibly memorized the scripture that says we are "saved by grace" (Ephesians 2:8), they sometimes pick up the notion that acceptance in the community of Christ is still based upon performance. And in some places that false belief is promoted; do right and God loves you, make a mistake and face his disapproval and judgment. But that is absolutely not the good news of the gospel. In fact, if what they say were true, it would simply be more bad news.

The message of the gospel is that at the cross Jesus has reconciled believers to God the Father. And now, united with him, the resources of the Kingdom belong to the children of faith. Having been united with Jesus and reunited with the Father, every Christian man, woman, and child is able to rest secure in the love and generosity of God. Granted, that is not easy to believe, especially for the emotionally wounded. Old messages and deep wounds can keep people, like me, closed off from feeling the lavish grace of God. There are still times when I have a hard time moving what I know to be true in my head down into what I feel in my heart. I need help from the Holy Spirit to integrate the reality of God's unmerited favor into how I respond to him emotionally. But, again by his grace, I am increasingly experiencing the joy of being fully accepted by God because of the sacrifice of Jesus at Calvary.

A follower of Christ stands righteous before the Father. How? By the grace of God, received by faith. The believer is indwelt by the Holy Spirit and transformed into the likeness of Jesus. How? Once again the answer is grace. A disciple of Jesus has been given spiritual gifts, can walk and minister in the power of the Holy Spirit, live in the light of God's love, and experience a peace that passes all understanding. These too are given freely by God's grace. When Christians make mistakes they do not need to fear God's judgment or rejection, because by God's grace the punishment was placed on Jesus. It is God's grace that enables stumbling Christians to rise again and move forward toward holiness and freedom. And when believers pass from this life to the next, they will enter heaven, a place of eternal joy and communion with God and the saints, all by the rich and lavish generosity of God's grace. These gifts are not earned, but freely given because of Jesus. And though it may be difficult for broken people to touch this grace at a feeling level, it is true just the same. And over time, through the process of emotional healing, people will begin to experience the power of this grace and begin to feel a love that defies description.

What does this discussion of grace have to do with traumatic wounding and the healing of memories? Just this. The person who walks that difficult path must never think that the promised freedom of God comes only to those who are good enough, who do enough, and who sare willing to earn his favor. That is not the way of the Kingdom of God. Being united with Father God, being set free from the ravages of traumatic wounding, and being able to live in the light of his love are gifts. They are lavish gifts that God has made possible through Jesus and that can be received by all who place their faith in him and cry out for his help.

I am not saying that broken people do not play a part, for they do. Wounded believers must face the places of darkness and pain, and be willing to release the pent up and unprocessed feelings that remain locked within. Rather than running away, they must move into those dark memories. That is not an easy process, and will involve time and energy. As already stated, I am still moving into the damaged places of my wounded past. But the wonder and beauty of Christ in all of this is that he will meet willing people in the places of darkness, fear, and pain.

Jesus will take broken people by the hand and walk us through the traumatic wounding and into new life. Jesus does this not because people have earned it, but because he gave his blood on Calvary for them and for that level of deep transformation. That is what the grace of God is all about, and it is for you, and me, and every person walking the face of the earth. This grace flows from the heart of God who loves his children with an everlasting and lavish love.

God's Love

While most Christians mentally grasp the notion of grace, it can be difficult connecting emotionally with a loving God. More than once I have prayed with people about inviting God into their wounded past and the initial reaction has been quite negative. When I ask people how they feel about God coming close to them, they use words like fearful, anxious, hesitant, and insecure. They understand the concept of a loving God as a propositional truth, but fear that in reality he is angry, judgmental, withholding, and punitive. Thus they are hesitant, even resistant, to invite God into places of pain and brokenness. This reluctance is the result of distorted god-images that were deeply ingrained, often at a very early age. Experiences with parents, the church, and life unfortunately caused a negative view of God to develop, which keeps people in bondage. Those distorted images need to be revealed and healed so that people can begin to actually experience the love of God that will set them free.

Recently I was reflecting on a distorted god-image that I had as a little boy, which negatively impacted my attitude toward God even into adulthood. I remembered walking out of my bedroom at about five years old, entering the living room and seeing my mother watching Billy Graham on television. We were not a particularly religious family and watching a television program about anything spiritual was out of character for anyone in my family. As I entered the room Billy Graham was talking about the second coming of Christ. Within minutes of being there I experienced a terror and panic that was overwhelming. I immediately ran back to my room and tried to do something to get that picture and those words out of my mind. It took days for me to regain a sense of stability, and I can say in no uncertain terms that Billy Graham was definitely not a safe person!

My reaction was not really to Billy Graham. I was afraid of God and anything that had to do with him. And that fear was based on a distorted view of God that was regularly communicated to my sister and me by my mother. Her own story of being orphaned and abandoned as a child is quite sad. One result of that wounding was that my mother needed a world that was in order and under control. And one way she accomplished that with my sister and me was by regular statements that mistakes or disobedience would be met not only with her disfavor, but with the punishment of God.

In our home, God was often portrayed as an exacting, angry authority figure who met disobedience with wrath. More than once I was reminded that God could "get me" if I was not a good boy. I am sure that my mother, raised in part in a strict German environment, was herself damaged by this caricature of God. And over the years she has been learning that God is an accepting Father who extends lavish love to the broken. But as a young mother she unfortunately portrayed God as stern and quick to punish. The impact upon me, and in turn my sister, was certainly deep and damaging.

My earliest experiences in church were little different. There seemed to be an almost sadistic preoccupation with hell and damnation by some preachers. I remember as a teen being taken to a youth crusade to hear a popular preacher at Carnegie Hall in Pittsburgh. My motivation for attending was the presence of pretty girls, but in the end I got more than I bargained for. The sermon was on the sword of the Lord that was going to come through the land. I remember the fear that overwhelmed me and at the invitation to be saved from hell I rushed forward. I was scared to death. At one level I am sure that a work of God was done in my heart that night, though it would be years before any positive fruit was seen. But my fear of the God of wrath was deeply reinforced.

With such a distorted image of God, who would ever willingly expose weakness and vulnerability before him? The idea of being honest about my frailties seemed like an invitation to more pain. And trusting that God would be tender toward me about my wounded past was impossible to comprehend, even as an adult employed in full time Christian service. That distrust was only reinforced by years of struggle with emotional disorders. Deep within I questioned how a loving God could ever allow me to experience such long term and debilitating pain. My interaction with a God who could be trusted unconditionally seemed limited at best.

The image of God that shaped my attitude was characterized by sternness, anger, and wrath. And until that was challenged at an experiential level, little would change. My experience with many other wounded people tells me that I am far from alone. While at an intellectual level the majority of Christians would say that God is love, at a primitive emotional level they fear that God is not loving and patient and they resist the invitation to turn to him with life's greatest hurts.

But God, in his tender grace, has been willing to help me surrender distorted images that have kept me in fear. Through the patient help of the Holy Spirit I am growing to embrace the true and living God of Love. While the process has taken time, the results have been wonderful and very freeing. Step by step, building upon small but important experiences of his love, I have been able to increasingly feel the delight of God for me. Old caricatures of God are passing away, and a new experience of his love is taking shape. Much of this change has come by allowing the Lord to heal wounds of childhood. Allowing Christ to enter places of deep pain and there to extend unconditional acceptance and love has enabled me to discover the Father's heart. Far from judgmental and punitive, I have found him to be welcoming, accepting, and generous with love. I certainly have not entered the rest that his love affords, but I am moving toward it.

My favorite text about the love and tenderness of God comes from Isaiah 42. It is a poetic description of the ministry of Christ, who comes as God's servant to save the broken and battered of this world:

> Here is my servant, whom I uphold, my chosen one in whom I delight; I will put my Spirit on him and he will bring justice to

the nations. He will not shout or cry out, or raise his voice in the streets. A bruised reed he will not break, and a smoldering wick he will not snuff out. (Isaiah 42:1-3)

Shouting, force, and punishment were certainly characteristics of the god I was introduced to as a child. But here, Isaiah speaks of the true God, who in tenderness and compassion sends his servant, Christ, to help wounded people everywhere. He does not shout, but instead gently ministers to the smoldering wicks and bruised reeds of the world. Later, in that same chapter, the Lord tells Isaiah that he wants to take his people by the hand, connect with them deeply, open blind eyes, free imprisoned captives, and release all those who sit in dungeons of darkness (Isaiah 42: 6 and 7).

God restates his mission of compassion and mercy in Isaiah 61 as the Lord's Servant declares:

The Spirit of the Sovereign Lord is upon me, because the Lord has anointed me to preach *good news to the poor*. He has sent me to *bind up the brokenhearted*, to proclaim *freedom for the captives* and *release from darkness* for prisoners, to proclaim *the year of the Lord's favor* and the day of vengeance of our God, *to comfort all who mourn*, and *provide for those who grieve* in Zion – *to bestow on them a crown of beauty* instead of ashes, *the oil of gladness* instead of mourning, and *a garment of praise* instead of a spirit of despair. They will be called *oaks of righteousness*, a planting of the Lord for the display of his splendor. (Isaiah 61: 1-3)

Jesus read this text in the synagogue of Nazareth at the beginning of his ministry, identifying himself as the Servant promised by God those many centuries before (Luke 4:14-19). Jesus came in love and tenderness to heal the hurting and free those who were trapped in the prisons of spiritual and emotional darkness. He came as a living demonstration of the Father's heart for broken people everywhere.

Jesus, who is God's Son, came to demonstrate in word and deed what the true and living God was really like. Simply stated, Jesus, through his many healings, deliverances, acts of kindness, and deeds of mercy, proved that God is love! In the first century the broken rushed to be close to Jesus, asking if they could touch him or at least touch his clothes in order to experience the healing power of God's love. And, according to scripture, when they did reach out to Jesus they were miraculously healed (Mark 6:56).

One of the greatest stories ever told is that of the prodigal son, recorded in Luke 15. Jesus told this parable to illustrate the wonderful and welcoming nature of God the Father toward even the worst of his children. In this story a rebellious young son asks his father for his inheritance, impatient to wait for his father's death. Taking the money, he goes away and wastes it on wild living, until he is penniless and destitute. Broken, he limps toward home with hopes that his father will at least receive him as a common servant. But the father, constant in love, sees the son coming and runs to him in great joy, embraces him, and receives him without condition. He kills the fatted calf for a celebration, gives him a ring of authority and blessing, and rejoices in the son who was once lost, but is now secure in his arms again.

Jesus told this parable to make it clear that God is not an ogre in the sky, but instead a welcoming Father, anxious to receive all who turn to him in brokenness and need. This scandalous grace was then, and in many places still is, hard for many religious people to accept. Knowing this, Jesus included in the parable an elder son who is angered by the father's generosity and grace, himself living out of a grace-less philosophy of works righteousness. Many in the community of faith are like that, wanting to control people through fear and demands for right behavior. But Jesus, by his life and teachings, demonstrates that God is not like that at all. The Father is full of grace, lavish in love, and tenderly accepts into his arms the wounded and broken of this world.

This brings me back to those precious people—possibly like you and definitely like me—who struggle with the debilitating affects of traumatic wounding. God cares immeasurably, and He has made a way of help in Jesus Christ. He is willing, and certainly able, to enter the pain of the unprocessed past and help people resolve the conflicts that rage within their minds and hearts. Through the ministry of the Holy Spirit, Jesus can help the broken release the pent up emotions of deep trauma and He can heal the wounds of long ago. Regardless of the level of disorder or debilitation, Christ is compassionate, and powerful, and longs to touch the hearts of all who turn to Him. I have experienced that healing touch in the past, and am even now positioned for more freedom that comes in the name of Jesus. Later in this book I will discuss a way to position the broken for just such an encounter with the Lord.

Turning to God for help is critically important for all people, no more so than those men and women who are on that journey "not of their own choosing." Many contemporary secular traumatologists, behavioral scientists, and leading psychologists are writing today about the role God plays in setting people free from PTSD and other psychological disorders. Granted, their concepts of God are not always consistent with the testimony of scripture. But even so, they are increasingly aware that no amount of talk therapy or self-help will ever actually set a person free.

It takes a greater power than is available through human will and understanding to set a prisoner free. Healing and transformation only occur in the hands of God, who has extended his love as wide as the outstretched arms of Christ on Calvary. Even now, through his good Spirit, the Father is beckoning the "smoldering wicks" and "bruised reeds" of this world to experience the transforming power of his unconditional and everlasting love. He is willing to take broken people by the hand and walk with them into the memories of past traumatic events. God in Christ is the wounded healer, full of grace and love, and extends to all an offer of ever increasing transformation and freedom.

Chapter Two

THE WATER IS TOO DEEP

In 1954 my parents bought a small three bedroom house in a rapidly developing, post-World War II, suburban neighborhood. The cost of the average home in the development was about ten thousand dollars, and houses were being sold as fast as they could be built. It was the baby boom and young families were moving into the area to find jobs in the coal mines and steel mills. My father was a miner and this new home was unquestionably the best house Dad and Mom had ever lived in. They are still in that house today, more than fifty years later. The only difference is that the house has been remodeled over the years, and the neighborhood has far more senior citizens than it does children.

My sister Bonny and I grew up in that Roman brick home, surrounded by dozens of kids our age. On our street alone there lived well over forty children, with more moving into the developing side streets all the time. After a couple of years, my dad's mother and stepfather moved next door, along with dad's sister Peg and my cousin Sandy. The newly developing neighborhood was rising up out of what had been a farmer's field, so trees were few and the surroundings were plain. But there was plenty of good dirt to play in and not far away was a wooded lot where the gang of boys spent many summer days playing army in our dad's discarded uniforms.

Most families were struggling financially in our neighborhood, with steel mill workers and coal miners making below average wages, and on strike as much as they were on the job. None of my friends' families were any better off than we, living a good basic life without a lot of extras. Most kids made do with second-hand bikes and hand-me-down clothes, and everyone lived on the same economic level—that is, everyone except the family who lived across the street and two doors up, Mr. and Mrs. Philpot.

The Philpots, unlike the other couples on our street, were close to retirement and had no children living at home. By the standards of most of my friends and their parents, it appeared as though the Philpots had money. Their house was built on a double lot, larger and constructed of stone instead of brick, and they drove a Chevrolet Impala convertible. Most impressively for a kid in the suburbs, they had an in-ground swimming pool that was hidden behind a solid wood fence.

The Philpots did not allow any of the neighborhood kids to swim in their pool, so for well over a dozen years all I knew was that there was a pool behind their fence, but I had never actually seen it. One day, while home from college for the summer, I saw Mrs. Philpot at Dubbs' Grocery Store, and she told me to feel free to come over and swim anytime. That very afternoon I decided to take her up on her offer. It turned out to be a very memorable day.

Upon returning from the store I discovered that my sister, who was married and living in another town, was visiting. So I invited Bonny to come along swimming with me at the Philpot's. It was wonderful, walking behind that solid wooden fence and seeing the pool for the very first time. Even better was the fact that no one was there, so the pool was all ours. I hurriedly jumped in the water, while Bonny found a body raft and soon joined me. Swimming was great fun to me, but what I did not know at the time was that my sister did not know how to swim. She got into the shallow end, mounted the raft, and began floating around the pool, all the time being no more that an arm's length from the side. Bonny was nervous, but did not want me to know.

Being a typical brother, I splashed Bonny and threatened to dunk her, even though we both knew I wouldn't. She was a good sport about it all, but definitely less than enthusiastic. At one point, while I was swimming at the other end, Bonny strayed from the side of the pool and, without my seeing, began to panic. In her desperation to grab the side she fell off the raft and it floated out of her reach.

When I looked over at Bonny, she was beating at the water frantically. Unaware of what was really going on, I started to splash her, thinking it was all fun. But her reaction told me in no uncertain terms that she was truly frightened. From my perspective this was no big deal. All she had to do was take a couple strokes and she would be at the side of the pool. I told her she was would be fine as I made my way toward her, to which she screamed, "I'm not fine, I'm drowning. The water is too deep!" Bonny's head went under the water just as I grabbed her arm and pulled her toward me. She had been fighting for air, close to drowning and I did not even know it.

The relief on Bonny's face as I helped her from the pool was easy to see. Once out, she went to one of the lounge chairs and collected herself. She told me repeatedly how frightened she had been, and how great it felt to be out of the water. I assured her everything was fine and we even spent a few moments in nervous laughter. But one thing was clear, no matter how hard I tried to persuade her, Bonny was not getting back in the water. She had enough and was contented right were she was. When we got home, she told the story to my folks more than once, repeating each time that she had never been so scared, and when out of the water, never felt so good.

A Perfect Metaphor

I have never forgotten that day in the Philpots' pool, grateful that everything turned out well. But what happened there serves as a perfect metaphor for what it is like to struggle with an emotional disorder brought on by traumatic wounding. People who have been the victims of painful events in the past often become hyper-vigilant and extremely sensitive to their environment, with a constant undercurrent of anxiety. Experience tells them that at any time the "water" that comes with life could suddenly get too deep. Those who have battled psychological disorders know how powerful negative emotions can, without warning, flood in and capsize them. And these fast moving waters can be unleashed by what would seem to most people a small, normal stress that is easily handled. When that deluge begins things get bad fast and it becomes hard to get air. Panic and terror quickly set in and people feel as if they are going to drown in the rush of pent up emotional pain.

Most people who witness this are perplexed. From their perspective nothing is wrong or threatening. The person who is struggling is just overreacting, or so it seems. And so friends, family, and even caregivers try to reason with the struggling person, explaining that everything is fine and can be faced with a minimum of effort. They wonder why something as harmless as a life-splash could evoke such an over-reaction. They do not realize that the person is suddenly experiencing far more stress than that brought on by the actual situation. The normal life-event has tapped into an ocean of unprocessed emotional pain from previous traumatic wounding and it is literally overwhelming. They feel as if they are out of control and sinking fast.

Knowing that emotional suffocation can happen without warning, wounded people are careful to have at least one life raft ready at all times, one safety vest that will support them when the emotional waters get too deep to handle. They try to stay as far away from deep water as possible, staying where they can get a firm hold on something solid. If some event or place has capsized them in the past, they will be very hesitant to place themselves in that situation again. Broken people often falsely believe that avoidance is a way to protect themselves from future problems with emotional floods. And their world keeps getting smaller as a result. But for those who have gasped for air in a rising emotional storm, all the while trying not to drown, a smaller world does not seem so bad. At least they can breathe.

A View from the Inside Out

I can easily share a dozen examples of being suddenly locked in an emotional episode rooted in an unprocessed past that suddenly floods into my today. And each time the experience is very much like the events that took place at the Philpots' pool. I can get stuck in emotional overload by a variety of triggers, and there is really no telling how long it will last or how bad it will get. It can be anything from a distressing hour to days or weeks of struggle. During such times my emotions are intense and all over the board. I begin to be hypervigilant about everything, misinterpret what is going on around me, and send myself many unhelpful messages. If it is an episode I cannot easily shake, I begin to withdraw from people and stressful situations, avoiding anything I think might make things worse than they already are. Most people do not know the intensity of what is happening inside me, because fearing embarrassment and shame I keep it hidden away as much as possible. And in the past, even if I did feel safe enough to share, few people ever understood.

Allow me to be more specific by sharing an actual example. My wife Cheryl and I were spending time in South Carolina. We have a home there that is in a restful setting and close to the beach. While there our son Aaron and his two daughters, Grace and Addison, came to spend a week with us while Aaron's wife, Destry, was teaching at a prayer retreat. As always with our children and grandchildren, the time together was wonderful. Aaron and the girls were great fun, full of life and love, and gave lots of hugs and kisses. It was a delightful week and I felt great. I was free from any nagging anxiety, and excited to spend every possible minute with Cheryl, Aaron and the girls. We played together every day, went for walks on the beach, watched children's movies at night, and ate plenty of sugar-free ice cream. Papa was experiencing a bit of heaven on earth.

After a week, the time came for Aaron and the girls to return to Ashland, Ohio, where we all live. Cheryl and I are one of those blessed set of parents who, after some years separated geographically from our older children, are now surrounded by all our kids. They all live close to us and we can see them virtually every day. So the separation from Aaron and the girls was only temporary, and we were free to return home ourselves whenever we chose. I say all that to provide a context for what happened to me when they left.

Cheryl and I hugged and kissed the kids, said our good-byes, and watched them leave in the car on their journey home. Any parent in such a moment would feel some slight sadness, simply because it was so wonderful having them around. But as they began to leave, instead of normal sadness, I began to experience waves of deep grief and a desperate longing to have them with me again. They had not been gone five minutes, and I was overwhelmed emotionally with their leaving. And with that I began to move into an episode of emotional flooding that lasted for almost three days.

The Waters Begin to Rise

As with each such episode, the first thing that happened was that I could not modulate my emotions. Initially I did not want Cheryl to know, so I told her that I was going for a walk. As I paced on the sidewalk outside I could sense that I was in trouble. Waves of sadness and grief were rolling over me and I could feel myself moving into that all too familiar emptiness of despair. I tried to give myself positive messages, but inside a part of me was not having any part of that. The anxiety began to build.

Prayers of desperation, begging God to help and not allow me to spin into this place, seemed to go nowhere. I was triggered and a flood of unprocessed feelings from past woundings was engulfing me. I felt deep grief, loneliness, and tremendous insecurity. I was working to push all this down, but it kept coming hard and fast. Panic began to emerge and I felt at the edge of losing control. I was frightened, angry, and deeply ashamed that I would be acting like this over something as normal and non-threatening as a brief time away from Aaron and the kids. But trying to stop the flood was like trying to hold back a tsunami. I just could not do it.

After a few hours of my private battle, Cheryl joined me outside so we could take our evening walk. As we did she noticed that I was silent and my body language signaled anxiety, which after all these years she picked up on immediately. As we walked she asked if I was alright, to which I responded that I was just missing the kids. Cheryl said that was normal, and she wished they did not have to go. And as we walked on, she began to talk about some of the fun things we had done together while they were here. And as she did, I could not hold back another minute. I started to cry, deeply. I was embarrassed, but could not hold back the flow of tears. I did not cry for a moment, but continually for the entire three mile walk. It was as if I were grieving a death. My heart was aching to be with the kids, as though I would never see them again.

The feelings did not subside with the crying, and throughout the next two days I was in a real battle. Angry over what was happening, I began to engage in tremendously negative self-talk. Instead of being patient and understanding with myself, I was brutal. In my mind I called myself a wimp, loser, sissy, and whatever other name I could think of to punish myself. I berated myself for being weak and out of control, disgusted that I was in this spot again, seemingly too frail to do anything about it. And my feelings of contempt were not limited to me. I wanted God to get me out of all this immediately, and for good. And yet he seemed silent and uninvolved, which angered me all the more.

Distorted Thinking

As anyone can guess by now, I do not think clearly when capsized by an unexpected flood of unprocessed emotions. In fact, my thinking gets distorted. As the waves of grief and sadness continued, I started telling myself I was losing my mind, that I was going to get mentally lost in this deep water. I was fighting for breath, and I thought I was going to drown. I felt as if I would never see my children again. I would die alone with no one there to even care.

My thoughts were irrational, welling up from the past and imposing themselves on the present situation, and this makes things very complicated and hard to figure out. That is what happens when people are caught in a post-traumatic episode. Their minds are overwhelmed by emotions from unprocessed traumatic past events, and they think irrational thoughts that are not based on the present reality.

As the waters continued to deepen, I began to develop a strategy to keep myself from being undone by it all. First, over the next two days I avoided as many of the places that reminded me of my time with the kids. Why? Because re-experiencing those moments would unleash more of the flood. I did not want to go sit out on the bench where Aaron and I had enjoyed several wonderful conversations.

Instead of returning to our favorite beach, I decided that Cheryl and I should try a new spot. The truth was that I did not want to be where Grace and I had played in the sand, because it would only mean more pain. I did not want to watch television, because that's what Addison and I did, with her snuggled up beside me.

On and on the strategy went. I was trying to run from pain by avoiding anything that would remind me of their time with me. Where normally such places would be a place of wonderful memories for a person, they had become for me potential triggers, and I did not want that. I was constructing a life raft to keep from drowning in all of this. And if that did not help, I was determined that we would just go home!

Help That Is Not Helpful

Over the years I have found that not all the help that people try to provide in a time like this is helpful. Their hearts are right, and from their perspective things are not that bad. They do not see a flood that threatens to capsize a person. It is, as they see it, a simple life-splash that is not a real threat at all. When I first began to battle such episodes I went to a counselor for help. I knew I could not walk this out alone, so I decided to humble myself and find a professional who understood what was happening and who would lead me to solid ground. In retrospect I now know that not all professionals understand traumatic wounding and unprocessed emotions from the past.

My counselor would have me describe what I was experiencing, and then work to give me new messages based on "reality." I remember as I was describing a similar incident that he said I was simply trapped in "stinkin thinkin." I simply needed to work at replacing bad thoughts with good thoughts. He wanted to help me see things as they really are, and he said that when I could do that I would not get caught in such emotional floods. In other words, he was telling me, as I did Bonny, that the situation was not really as bad as I thought and that with a bit of effort I could "get a grip."

But there was something my counselor did not understand, and thus was not able to help me. Emotional floods, like the one I was experiencing about Aaron and the kids, do not come from the present situation. That was simply the triggering event. Those powerful emotions come from unprocessed traumatic events of the past, and trying to address that with new thinking patterns relative to the triggering event misses the point. And it can be a tremendously frustrating process for the person experiencing these episodes. As hard as I tried to think about the present appropriately, I could not. Once triggered, I was caught in the past, and the only hope I had for healing was to be helped with identifying the actual origin of all this unprocessed pain, release it, and experience the healing of emotions through the power of Christ.

The Source of the Problem

So what was my reaction to Aaron and the grandchildren all about? It arose from a series of traumatic woundings that occurred when I was a child. As mentioned previously, my earliest childhood memories are of being terribly afraid. I well remember the horror of sleepless nights, trembling in my bed with the light on. It was not monsters or robbers that I feared were hiding beneath my bed. I was afraid of a dark emptiness that would seem to surround me, threatening to choke the life out of me. It felt as though I was smothering all alone, with some unidentifiable force trying to destroy me. For years I would sneak my way into my parents' room and try to climb in bed beside my mother. Many times she let me snuggle close, and there fall asleep. But this terror went on for years, and more often than not I was alone in my bedroom.

Back then, in the fifties, most parents did not take their children to a counselor for help. What I was experiencing was simply seen as something that a child would grow out of in time. Of course with me, that was long in coming. I remember being referred to as a "nervous child." My dad simply called it being a "momma's boy" which was embarrassing and shameful. I hated being called those things, and wanted to run away and hide. I became more and more alone in my private nightmare, hoping for the day when I would grow out of it as promised. But I never actually did grow out of it. During adolescence I was able to find a way to cope and kill the pain. But the anxiety never left by day, and by night it translated into a life-long battle with nightmares. What happens to me today, in situations like the one involving my son Aaron, is the adult version of what I remember experiencing even as a small child.

Beneath all this pain and emotion triggered by Aaron's leaving was some event or events that birthed the storm. But for years I never looked to the past for answers. I thought the problems were, as suggested by counselors, in the way I interpreted today. But, by God's wonderful love and care, the veil began to be lifted on my problems, and through the help of the Spirit and a couple of gifted friends, the source of the problem began to come to the surface. As yet, I am seeing through a glass dimly, but the picture is taking shape and the Lord is meeting me in the past to set me free.

I experienced a series of traumatic events before I was five years old. These included significant birth trauma, a severe burning on the entire right side of my face as a toddler, an experience of traumatic abandonment by my grandfather at three, and being present as he suddenly began to struggle and die from a brain abscess. During that same time my family went through the shooting of a relative. And, given my experience over the years, there was not any effort to process any of this. Not talking about difficult moments in life was my family's way of coping. As a result I have lived most of my life with great fear, and as an adult have been diagnosed with an attachment disorder and PTSD.

Through all the early years of battle, I did not once consider that the source of my problems was related to those early traumatic woundings. Instead, my problems were primarily identified, by me and others, as anything from being a "nervous child" or "momma's boy" to sinfulness or demons or chemical imbalance or bad diet or "stinkin thinkin." I am sure there have been such issues in my life. But the lifetime of emotional flooding that has repeatedly threatened to suffocate me has been about childhood trauma and the unprocessed emotions still present deep within my soul. It has not been the present but the past that has overwhelmed me. Freedom began as I took seriously the presence of a frightened child within who lives everyday afraid that he is going to, at any moment, find himself alone in the night facing sudden harm.

My natural tendency with difficult emotional times is to withdraw until everything stabilizes. It is a somewhat adult version of "growing out of it." But experience has taught me that it is far more helpful to engage with those who can help and allow them to walk me through the process of formational prayer. And there is no better time to do that than when actually stuck in an emotional episode like the one I have described involving Aaron. I am well aware that, as the person in the flood, my desire is to get on solid ground before dealing with the past issue. However, the process of healing actually progresses better if hurting persons allow Jesus to enter the deep water with them and process the pain of the past that is overwhelming them. Later I will not only share what that process involves, but will also discuss the kind of safety and support that is necessary, so that the wounded person feels secure enough to engage in the process.

The Rest of the Story

Here, I simply want to tell you the rest of the story. After almost three days of battle, I was able to connect by telephone with a dear and gifted friend, who has a keen understanding of traumatic wounding and a spiritual anointing for formational prayer. She has a unique ability to walk a broken person through to emotional healing in Christ. She listened compassionately as I told her the details of what was happening, and sensitively asked questions that would bring to the surface feelings and beliefs that pointed to an old, old wound deep within my soul.

When the time was right, she asked me to join her in prayer and began by helping me go within and find a safe place to be with Jesus. It is a process of using creative imagination that is based on scriptural truths. Following her guidance and with the Spirit's help, I was able to see myself on a wooden bench, with Jesus standing behind me with his hands tenderly touching my shoulders. I soon felt safe there, all the while still experiencing the overwhelming emotions of grief and abandonment.

My friend had me describe my negative feelings to the Lord, and as I did, I wept. Pent up feelings came rushing out, just as they had been doing for several days. At the appropriate moment, she directed me to ask the Lord to help me see the source of the pain. In time I was able to see myself as a small child, afraid, and alone in my room. The picture in my mind was of an actual event that occurred on a night long ago involving my dad and being left alone with intense fear.

In short, I was able to reenter that event with the Lord. Not only was I able to process the feelings I had related to it, I was able to sense the compassion of Christ and even see my "inner child" turn to Jesus in my childhood bedroom. I not only saw but sensed the Lord wrapping the four-year-old me in his robe. I was completely hidden in him, and the feelings of warmth and safety were overwhelming and wonderful. It was as if I were protected within a robe of light that felt like liquid love. I watched as Jesus spoke words of assurance, received the emotional pain into his heart, and promised the child part of me that even when no one else was there, he was. As the prayer time grew to a close, I was able to see not only myself on the bench with Jesus, but also that small child snuggled up with Jesus content and at rest.

It was a mysterious and spiritual encounter with Christ that brought undeniable release and healing. Even though none of the prayer was about Aaron or the grandchildren, the matter of his returning home was now in perspective. The present was secure because a past event was processed and no longer flooded into the moment. I now had the normal sense of regret about Aaron and the kids leaving. But it was no longer producing debilitating emotional upheaval. In fact, I was able to go immediately from there and sit on the very bench I had avoided and have pleasant memories of the time I spent there with my son. Likewise, I was able to remember the wonderful days I had with the kids, revisit our favorite beach without being triggered, and sit on the couch watching television and smile as I recalled Addi snuggled right at my side. Jesus had met me in the past in order to help me walk free in the present. He did not say, as others had, that the waters were not really as deep as I thought. Instead he drained away some unprocessed feelings from a painful wounding in my past. It was his gift of grace, a gift he gladly gives to all who meet him there. It is a healing gift I cherish and know I still need to experience in other, even deeper traumatic woundings that yet remain unprocessed.

Why Be So Vulnerable

The choice to be vulnerable about my own journey is not always met positively by others. It not only reveals my own soft underbelly, but it can and has positioned me for various levels of criticism. Even so, I feel compelled to be honest about my struggles with emotional wounding. I want to glorify the Lord, sharing openly about the grace that he gives me and is willing to extend to every broken person. Jesus has in the past and continues today to meet me in dark and painful places hidden deep within my soul. And through it all he does a work of healing and transformation that is real and lasting, and with each step along the way he draws me even closer to his loving heart.

It is amazing how much the church is uncomfortable with weakness and enamored with strength. But that is not the way of Christ or his kingdom. I have often thought about that in relationship to the way we remember people in scripture. Many of the people Jesus touched are actually identified by their weakness and need, not their strength or healing. We all have heard about the Gadarene demoniac, Blind Bartimaeus, the man with the withered hand, the woman caught in adultery, the woman with the portion of blood, and the leper who returned to thank Jesus. Yet, each and every one of them was set free from the very thing that now identifies them! The Gadarene "demoniac" has been delivered and in his right mind for over two thousand years. "Blind" Bartimaeus has not been blind since that day long ago when Jesus touched him. The "sinful woman" was forgiven, the "man with the withered hand" was healed, and the flow of blood forever stopped. And as for the leper, the priests declared him clean centuries ago.

Why do we still remember them for their weakness and need? It is because that is precisely where Jesus met them and forever trans-formed their lives. Rather than hide from their vulnerabilities and keep only strength in the light, Christians can find reason to praise God right from the places of their greatest weaknesses. That has cer-tainly been true for me. I once heard the companion of Corrie Ten Boom say that Corrie believed "The object of one's greatest pain can become the source of their greatest blessing when it is given to God." I have held that truth in my heart and have found it to be true. In the hands of Christ even traumatic wounds of the past can become places of life-changing blessing. And so, rather than hide my weaknesses, I am choosing to boast in them to the glory of the Healing Christ. I do not at all mind being known as the man who capsized in life, because that has become the very place where I have come to know Christ as never before.

There is another reason for choosing vulnerability. I know all too well the anguish and fear that accompanies emotional disorders. It can be a lonely journey, filled with deep pain and at times almost unbearable shame. Even in the community of Christ, the not too subtle message can be that "real Christians" do not have such prob-lems. This only makes those who struggle feel worse. My heart breaks for the broken, and if sharing my story helps even one, I am more than willing to be open and vulnerable about my own journey. If talking about my battle helps sustain someone through his or her own dark night, I will gladly shout it from the housetops, regardless of whatever negative reactions that may bring. The church has not had a history of being gracious toward those with emotional disorders. I want to see that change, and if by being open, others begin to extend more understanding and compassion to the hurting, it is certainly worth it all.

The Path to Healing

In recent years God has been equipping his people to help those who live with the effects of traumatic wounding. The work of people like Leanne Payne, David and Steve Seamands, Charles Kraft, Dennis and Matthew Linn, Sheila Fabricant, John and Paula Sandford, Siang-Yang Tan, and Ed Smith has had a powerful and positive effect on the people of God. I am deeply grateful to God for allowing me a small part in that process of change, and pray that my story will somehow help others see that there is hope and healing in Christ.

The path to healing always begins by recognizing the nature of the problem a person is facing. As seen in my own story, there are several characteristics that often come with the problem of unprocessed memories from past traumatic wounding. If you are wondering if you or someone you care about is facing this problem, consider the degree to which one is experiencing frequent times of:

Emotionally over-reacting to normal life stresses

Being unable to modulate feelings of fear, panic, and depression

Avoiding situations that may trigger a flood of emotions

Having difficulty thinking clearly about the situation and
potential responses

Withdrawing from life

Sending negative messages of self-contempt

Constructing various "life rafts" as a way of feeling safe

Even "healthy people" will find themselves experiencing any one
or two of these from time-to-time. This does not mean that they are
victims of past traumatic wounding. But when a person experiences
several of these on a consistent basis, there may in fact be a problem. That is the time to consider getting some help from someone
who understands what is taking place and can position the broken
for the healing of unprocessed memories. If you are seeking help, or
the person wanting to provide help, remember that this is no small
matter. It is critically important that a caregiver not only be spiritually
gifted for this ministry, but also trained and accountable.

Without proper training and supervision, a well intentioned person
can actually do harm to someone. That is why, as said earlier, this book
is written to help the broken find hope, and to better equip those who
help them. It is not a guide in itself for an untrained layperson who
wants to walk some friend or family member to healing. Any and all
caregivers intending to follow the guidance provided here must have
received adequate professional or advanced lay-level training. Apart
from that, no one should endeavor to actually move someone through
the process. That is important for both the person struggling and the
caregiver to know. An untrained member of the family or friend can
be a great source of prayer and support, which is absolutely essential
to the healing process. But without the proper instruction and experience, that should be the limit of their direct involvement.

Traumatic woundings happen all the time to people, and have
ever since time began. Yet most people do not understand what kind

of events are traumatic. Nor is there broad understanding of the effect they have upon people, and the reasons why some people are more impacted than others by the same type of event. That will be the focus of the next chapter.

Chapter Three

THE FACE OF TRAUMA

Mention that a person is struggling with the effects of a traumatic wounding from the past and most people think post-traumatic stress disorder. And if a person says post-traumatic stress disorder, many people assume it is the result of a catastrophic event like rape, assault or war. Invariably, if I share with an individual that I have battled post-traumatic stress, he or she asks me if I fought in Vietnam.

Just the other day I was sitting by the community pool at our home in South Carolina and a gentleman sat in the lounge chair next to me. I was writing notes on a yellow tablet and, wanting to begin a conversation, he asked what I was doing. I told him that I was pulling down some thoughts I might want to include in a book I was writing. His immediate response was, "What's it about?" I told him that it was about the effects of traumatic wounding and how to find healing in Christ. His immediate response: "I was in Vietnam too. I have PTSD and attend group three times a week." Truthfully, I was a little embarrassed to tell him that, not only had I not been in Vietnam, but that my own struggle was a result of events that happened to me as a child.

There is no doubt that fighting in a war and other catastrophic events are the cause of emotional disorders in many people. And in no way am I trying to minimize that fact. I have great respect for the men and women who have served in the military and fought to protect our freedom. I have on two occasions done seminars for the United States Army on the material presented here.

But there are many other, less obvious, events that happen to people every day that have a crippling effect on them emotionally. Unfortunately such wounds seem insignificant alongside rape, assault, and fighting in a war. As a result, those who have not experienced such highly stressful events dismiss the possibility that they could actually be suffering an emotional disorder from something that happened to them.

Mike is a middle-aged counseling student at a South Carolina University. We were talking one day and he mentioned that he was a recovering alcoholic and wanted to help others who were caught in that battle. At one point he mentioned that his counselor had diagnosed him with PTSD. He then quickly said, "I don't really believe him, because nothing really bad has ever happened to me, like being in a war or something."

I find that most people conclude that for an event to be traumatic it must be almost catastrophic in nature. While certainly this category of event does traumatically wound, other, less severe occurrences can have a crippling effect on those who experience them. Robert Scaer, in his book, *Trauma Spectrum: Hidden Wounds and Human Resiliency*, says that events that many in our culture define as "normal" can, over time, significantly traumatize people.[4] This is especially true of things that occur in the lives of infants and small children. Because most people do not consider such events as traumatic, they dismiss the possibility that their emotional struggles arise from unprocessed traumatic events of the past. In an effort to help people better understand the nature of such wounds, I have developed a simple, non-clinical typology of trauma. The five categories are:

Traumatic Wounds of Withholding in Childhood

Traumatic Wounds of Aggression in Childhood

Traumatic Wounds Caused by Stressful Events

Traumatic Wounds Caused by Betrayal

Traumatic Wounds Caused by Long Term Duress

I will define and discuss each in the following section.

In September of 2005 I conducted a seminar on formational prayer at the American Association of Christian Counselors. At one point in the presentation I went through each of the five categories of trauma. At the conclusion of each description I asked the following question: "How many of you, having heard this description, would say that you have experienced that type of trauma?" There were about 850 people in the session and at least three fourths of the people lifted their hands. I then asked, "And how many of you would say that to some significant degree that wounding continues to negatively effect the way you relate to yourself, others, and God?" Once again, three fourths of the people raised their hands. That happened after each description. At the end of the discussion I simply said, "Why is it that, given all that we know about counseling and psychology, we still struggle to this degree? I suspect that it is because we either do not take seriously what happened to us, or we have not yet learned how to invite Christ into our wounded pasts."

A Typology of Traumatic Wounding

There is certainly nothing profound about the following typology of wounding, but it may help people better understand the broad range of events that can traumatize people. I am providing it in hopes that it might encourage broken people to consider the possibility that their present emotional struggles may be directly related to unprocessed woundings of the past. And I am setting it forth to help caregivers better describe the nature and scope of traumatic events to people under their care. What follows is a detailed description of each category.

Traumatic Wounds of Withholding in Childhood

This designation refers to wounds that people experience as a result of not getting what they needed from the adults responsible for their care. Every child needs a great amount of attention and care to move through the early developmental stages of life successfully. The adults in their world are to provide nurture, sustenance, protection, and a place of safety for them. Infants and children need loving touch, words of affirmation, encouragement, and gentle instruction on their journey toward adolescence. They need to see delight in the faces of the adults who care for them, experience patience as they try new things, and hear words that build confidence, enabling them to take new risks in life. Children need big doses of hugs and kisses that communicate through the senses that they are special gifts to life. And foundational to all this is love unconditionally and generously given.

Most anyone would identify with this list and affirm that the infant/child who lives in an environment like that would have a great start in life. But what they would not readily admit is that the consistent absence of any one or combination of these can be a traumatic wounding that can affect the rest of their lives. In fact, some would actually protest the notion, saying that I was making way too much of a child not getting all he or she needs. After all, some might suggest, it will make children tougher in the end. However, tougher is not the goal; healthy is, and when these resources are withheld, it can have a tragic, long term effect.

Dennis and Matthew Linn share a story in their book, *Healing the Eight Stages of Life,* about the importance of love and touch for infant children. They write that at the turn of the 20th century an American pediatrician, Dr. Henry Chapin, had studied children's institutions in ten American cities. According to his findings, every child under two years old in all but one of these institutions died before reaching age two, regardless of the quality of medical care they received. Yet, in contrast, at the Children's Clinic in Dusseldorf, Germany, the mortality rate was the same as that of the general population.

Dr. Talbot, upon visiting the Children's Clinic, could not identify anything substantially different than that from the children's institutions in the United States. However, upon seeing an elderly lady moving through the clinic, he discovered that she, Old Anna, was given the task of mothering all the sick infants at Children's Clinic. She would pick them up, hold them, and give them the motherly love they needed. Without that love, the children often died. But receiving her love made the difference and helped them thrive.[5]

The resources of nurture listed earlier are essential to a child's development, and in some cases to survival. Failing to receive such care consistently can have a significant effect upon a child's ability, later in life, to feel confident, safe, and significant. It can negatively impact their relationships with other people, their ability to recover from difficult times, and their view of God. For some, these effects are significantly negative, and with others even severe. Such traumatic woundings must be taken into consideration when seeking to identify the source of a person's emotional upheaval. Too often a broken person, and even her caregiver, will pay exclusive attention to the present life situation, without considering the possibility of childhood woundings of withholding. To not receive nourishment and loving care is traumatic for a child, a life stress that goes beyond what is normal for that stage of life.

Traumatic Wounds of Aggression in Childhood

Thankfully there is increasing attention on the scope of this problem in our society today. These traumatic wounds are those that occur in children's lives because they received treatment they did not need. These are the wounds of physical, verbal, and sexual abuse. They also include the painful events of being abandoned, rejected, and treated with severity, whether intentionally or unintentionally. With wounds of aggression, some significant person has acted upon the child in a damaging way. And, as with all such traumatic wounds, the child then struggles through later life with the effects.

The nature and scope of these wounds is broad as well as deep. Nathan came to our church dressed as a woman and had a terrible time relating to men. He was forty six at the time and had spent most of his life hiding behind a woman's persona. Nathan was not struggling with sexual disorientation. He was terrified by men and did not want any level of relationship with anything masculine, even within himself. The sad story is that, abandoned by their mother, Nathan and his siblings were raised by their alcoholic father. As the oldest, Nathan was responsible for the behavior of all his siblings, beaten regularly by his father if any of them acted out of line while he was away. On several occasions he was locked in a closet for the night as punishment. He was deeply wounded by this abuse and it affected his entire life. Unfortunately, most Christians were far more concerned about Nathan's cross-dressing than they were his deep wounds. They did not take the time to hear his story and address the cause of his pain rather than the symptoms.

Far less abusive acts against a child can leave a lasting and damaging impact. My friend Summer struggled with obsessive behaviors for years, hyper-concerned that she did everything right, every time. This affected her relationship with her husband, children, and ultimately God. Upon looking for a possible root cause, Summer said that as a five-year-old child she was told that her mom and dad were divorcing and she could choose with whom to live. But privately her father told her that if she chose him, her mother would stay and they would not divorce. She chose to go with her mother, and the divorce occurred, a fact her father often blamed on her.

Abusive behavior toward children is traumatic for them, whether it happens sexually, physically, or verbally. Countless people are adult victims of such cruel behavior. If a person can be guided properly to recognize traumatic wounding, he or she can find release and healing from emotions and behaviors that have been damaging. Hurtful words like, "you're stupid" or "you never do anything right" may not seem like a big deal, especially as they are compared to events like molestation and physical abuse; but in truth they are a big deal, with some children more so than others.

People who recognize that they received this type of treatment, should prayerfully consider the effect it has had upon them. An ongoing struggle with confidence, self-image, connecting with others, and fear of God can find roots in just such traumatic woundings. The good news is that Jesus is present, not only in today, but in yesterday as well. He is willing to meet people in those memories and ultimately set them free.

Traumatic Wounds Caused by Stressful Events

Earlier I shared that as a small child I was present when my grandfather experienced a brain abscess that took his life. Over fifty years later I still remember that event. I was standing in the corner of my grandparents' kitchen, when suddenly I heard my grandfather scream in the other room. I was frozen in fear, almost unable to breath. I watched as my Aunt ran horrified to find him. In moments she was helping my grandfather struggle to the bathroom, which was only a few feet from where I was standing. There was terror on both of their faces. He was throwing up, falling, losing consciousness. I was in sheer panic. I had no idea what was happening. I did not understand the loud shouting, the screams of pain, or the look on my grandfather's face. My aunt shut the door to the bathroom, and that was the last time I ever saw him.

Within moments my step-grandfather arrived and took my cousin and me away. No one ever explained what was happening, helped me process all the pain, or even brought the subject up again. Grandpap was gone. I was not taken to the funeral. All that fear, terror, and loss were locked inside me. While the traumatic event was unavoidable, what followed, or better said, what did not follow, was not. It was negligent to not help a four-year-old child deal with all that pain and confusion. It undoubtedly accounts for at least part of why I battle PTSD today. But nothing was said, and life just went on as normal— except that I was far less normal as a result. And, as already discussed in the previous chapter, years of emotional struggles were never linked to what happened to me so long ago. And since the vast majority of the counseling I received focused on the present, little changed.

From conception to the grave people can experience traumatic woundings that rock their world. Event trauma knows no age limit, respects no status, and issues no warning. Whether through accident, sudden illness, or sweeping catastrophe, people can find themselves suddenly wounded by an uninvited event. It may be a national catastrophe, like the downing of the Twin Towers, or Hurricane Katrina, or the tornados that devastated Gallatin, Tennessee. Event trauma comes in all shapes and sizes, and often leaves a lasting limp in people's ability to walk through life successfully.

I have a dear friend, who will remain unnamed, who was assigned to help identify body parts in the rubble of the Trade Center disaster. He was deployed with his local police unit and willingly served as assigned. He is a dear man and a wonderful Christian. He knows the sustaining power of Christ, and has leaned on him many times in life. And yet, one afternoon, several days into his assignment, he had seen enough. Something inside his mind said, "No more," and he began to struggle emotionally. The event had traumatized him and he was in trouble. Upon returning home he could not sleep, and when he did he battled constant nightmares. Ultimately, he had to go for treatment because, even motivated by a desire to help, what he saw and did was too much and he entered a difficult battle with PTSD.

I grew up watching many westerns and war movies, and the impression one gets is that real men can face anything and remain unaffected. But that is a myth. It is different in real life. Certain events, stressful beyond what is normal, can impact the strongest of people. Many individuals in our society struggle at various levels because of something traumatic that they witnessed or experienced. And there is no shame in admitting that fact. Being honest about the impact event trauma has had is the first step to being free. And it is important for the wounded and those who care for them to remember: Jesus experienced great trauma beginning soon after his birth and continuing through to the cross. He stands ready to meet anyone and everyone in the painful place of the past.

Traumatic Wounds Caused by Betrayal

Some might argue that betrayal trauma could be included within the previous category and that might be true. But given my definition, it is significant enough to be listed as a separate type of traumatic wounding. Betrayal trauma occurs when a person or persons violate the position of power they hold over someone in their care. It can and often does involve other types of wounding behavior, but betrayal trauma stands as a significant violation by itself. Regardless of the form it takes, this type of wounding can profoundly damage a person's trust and can give birth to deep insecurity. Betrayal trauma can happen at the hands of parents, teachers, pastors, priests, physicians, counselors, psychologists. It is trauma that occurs because a person is under the care of someone who abused power and ended up hurting them.

I was invited to speak to the college class of Neighborhood Church in Redding, California. They were on retreat in the mountains, a short drive from our home in Palo Cedro. The theme was "Experiencing Intimacy with Jesus," and I was given a morning to share on that topic. The students met in a large loft of a log home, and were spread out across the floor to listen to what I had to say. They were attentive, interested, and very respectful to me—that is, except for one red haired young man they called Brick. Throughout the first session he would not stop disrupting, either talking loudly or asking loaded questions trying to induce an argument. During the break the leaders apologized, telling me that Brick was always like that and they had tried everything to get him to behave. I thanked them for their concern and entered the session excited about the topic and the opportunity to share.

The second session was like the first, with Brick stirring the pot. After one particularly disrespectful remark, I said, "Brick, some authority figure in your life must have hurt you badly, and I am sorry about that. It should never have happened." The room was in stunned silence, and the leaders had anxiety written all over their faces. Brick just stared at me, and as I stood there quietly, tears began to slowly well up in his eyes. I then said, "Do you want to talk about it?" While I intended the conversation to be private, Brick began to tell his story.

Brick's betrayal had happened when he was just a child in his kindergarten class. Apparently his teacher was an atheist and Brick's mom had unfortunately told him that she was going to hell. Brick had, as children will do, said that to his teacher. That comment gave birth to a year long experience of rejection and abuse. The teacher, who was an adult, made it her business to go head to head with this child, punishing Brick for repeating what he heard at home. Brick said that it was the worst year of his life, and that he hated school, and teachers, and authority figures ever since, and understandably so. He had been violated and was never given the opportunity to process the pain. The youth leaders saw only Brick's disrespect and worked to straighten him out. But the source of the problem was a traumatic betrayal from the distant past.

Abuse of power is a serious issue and needs to get more attention, particularly in the church. Most believers are preoccupied with sexual sin, and granted it is a serious problem. But, as I once said to my students, there is some chance that they, as pastors, will commit sexual sin; but there is a great chance that they will abuse power. And when they do, someone will be deeply hurt and it could affect their level of trust and security for the remainder of their lives.

Traumatic Wounds Caused by Long Term Duress

Alice came to one of our retreats seeking release from serious seasons of despair and an eating problem. She was extremely over weight and as a result was facing numerous health problems. Alice had withdrawn from most of her friends and, worse, believed that God had abandoned her. The only reason she came was because a friend paid her tuition and brought her to the event. When Alice arrived her countenance was fallen and everything about her communicated deep sadness and loss. She was tired, filled with self-contempt, and had given up hope. It was obvious that she had experienced some type of deep wounding. The question was, "What kind of traumatic experience was at the root of it all?"

Alice was relatively disengaged through much of the retreat, yet God was faithful and opened a way for her to be deeply touched by his grace. During one of the sessions Alice told the group that several times a day for twenty years, her husband referred to her as a fat, mother f___ing pig. Her words not only shocked everyone in the room, they enraged them. Several spoke openly and with passion about how terrible and wrong this brutality was. She simply replied, "Its okay, I guess that's what I really am."

Alice was a victim of wounding caused by long term duress. Duress is defined as negative stress that disempowers people. It is the water torture of trauma. A single moment of negative stress can be hurtful, exhausting, and draining. But for most people short term duress will not have a long term effect. If Alice's husband had insensitively said those words to her in an angry moment one time, and then humbly apologized for his bad behavior, the pain would have eventually passed. But those same words, spoken in anger every day over an extended period of time, would take a heavy toll on anyone. It certainly did on Alice. She needed to receive formational prayer and clear guidance on how to set boundaries with abusive people.

Long term exposure to duress affects a person like drops of water falling on granite. A few drops will evaporate without having any significant impact. But if the dripping continues long enough, it will wear down even the strongest person. Whether it is prolonged seasons of opposition, criticism, physical pain, isolation, or any of countless other pressures, it can deeply wound most anyone. That is particularly true if long term duress occurs to children. It can be devastating to their development, crippling them for life. And sadly, not everyone takes prolonged duress seriously, and so it goes unchallenged and its effects unaddressed.

The typology of traumatic wounding discussed in this section was designed to help people understand the wide range of hurtful events that people experience in life. Many people are victims of each type and at some level struggling with the effects. The following section discusses the actual impact of traumatic experiences on people, ranging anywhere from insignificant to life altering.

The Effects of Traumatic Events

Simply stated, people react differently to traumatic experiences. It would be helpful if that were not true, but it is. Two people can go through exactly the same situation and for one it has little long term effect, yet for the other it is deeply wounding. For many people who struggle with traumatic wounding, the fact that some people seem to get through it without serious problems can produce shame. They often conclude that they are simply weaker than others and should be able to "get over it." It can lead to more than a little self-contempt and self punishment. However, differences in how an event impacts people are driven by far more than a person's will to move beyond a bad situation.

Through my reading, discussions with psychologist friends, and personal experience, I have learned that a combination of factors influence the difference between people's varying responses to the same type of traumatic experience. In part the difference can be related to the age of the person when experiencing the event. Seeing a grandparent die is traumatic regardless of one's age, but it is highly likely that, all things being equal, it will have a more devastating effect upon a small child than an adult. The adult has more life experience and personal resources to draw from than a small child, and for this reason would probably handle it better. Individual personality types can also impact responses to traumatic events. People have different temperaments and therefore react to events and process them in different ways. For example, some people are external processors who resolve inner tensions by talking with others, which is helpful. But others process internally, and are likely to try to resolve tensions in isolation. This is most often not helpful, actually impeding the journey of recovery.

Another factor that can determine the impact a traumatic event has upon an individual is how those close to the individual respond to the situation. When acceptance, care, compassion, and concern are openly expressed a healing presence is created by those close to the traumatized person. This presence enhances recovery. But if those closest respond with distance, rejection, shame, denial, or judgment, the impact can be far greater and more devastating. In addition, the meaning attached to the event greatly impacts the degree to which a traumatic event effects a person. Event trauma is serious in itself, but the conclusions being drawn from the event affect the long term impact. A car accident, for example, demands a season of emotional and physical recovery regardless. But if someone concluded from such an event that driving or riding in a car is always dangerous, that person will most often have a much harder time recovering than the person who determines that accidents can and do happen but do not categorically mean that traveling is always a high risk activity.

The Attachment Bond

Several of the leading people who research this issue have concluded that the number one factor that impacts a person's response to a traumatic event is the security of their attachment bond as an infant.[6] People who were deeply loved by their parents, nurtured, and delighted in during the early months of life seem to be endowed with a deeper resilience and strength. The care of the parent at that age, and their responses to the child's wants and needs, have a determining effect upon the future of that child. According to many people who are specialists in treating the effects of trauma, those infants who bond deeply during the earliest months of life simply do better.

Knowing this should impact us in several ways. First, as adults we need to do everything possible to draw little ones into our arms, look into their faces, and communicate the greatest delight imaginable. We need to love children as actively as possible, because their futures depend on it. When a child comes running to us when hurt, we should sweep them up into our arms, look them in the face with eyes of love and calmness, and let them know everything will turn out fine. Children need this if they are to respond well in life. Given the importance of this issue, it is little wonder that Jesus welcomed children and called them the blessed of his kingdom. Secondly, we must take seriously the importance of connecting broken adults to a community of believers. Experiences of love have a great impact on the healing process, and those who have been hurt need to re-experience attachment to people who will genuinely and actively care about them. Connecting is essential to recovery.

Finally, those of us who are almost embarrassed that we have limped through life because of what happened to us as a child need to accept a basic truth: the failure to experience bonding, love, and nurture as an infant is a wounding of the worst kind. For a parent not to throw themselves into the nurture and development of an infant, who enters this world completely vulnerable and filled with need, is one of life's greatest violations. Whether intentional or not, failure to bond with an infant wounds that person for the rest of life. It is life's most tragic example of how the actions of another can ravage the life of an innocent person. Thankfully, through the Father love of God, and the extended arms of the Christ of Calvary, there is a way of healing for us all.

Distortion

Traumatic events not only affect some people and not others, they can wound people in different ways and to different degrees. To help people understand that, I place the nature of negative effects into two different categories, *distortion* and *disorder*. The first, distortion, is significant, yet less severe than disorder. The term represents what often happens to people who have been impacted by wounding. The event distorts the way they see the world and react to life. For all intents and purposes they are able to function, hold jobs, build relationships, and experience life as most others would. The wound has created problems for them that are painful and unhealthy, but they would not be diagnosed as having a clinical problem. All the same, the traumatic wounding is keeping them in some level of bondage and dysfunctional behavior.

In *Healing Care, Healing Prayer,* I wrote about a cause and effect relationship between wounds and responses. It is illustrated as follows.

Life Situation

Dysfunctional Behavior

Emotional Upheaval

False Belief

Wound

When people are *wounded* in life—either by a traumatic event or less stressful experience—it does far more than cause initial pain. It often negatively impacts what they believe about themselves, their world, and God. Those *false beliefs*, in turn, create powerful feelings that chronically stir within, bringing significant discomfort to their lives. That *emotional upheaval* is unsettling, and over time not always consciously linked to the internal false beliefs. But the discomfort is significant and, as a result, people engage in a wide variety of *dysfunctional behaviors* designed to kill the emotional pain. Those dysfunctional, sinful responses to the internal feelings are acted out in their daily lives.

Imagine for a moment that when you were a teenager, your father repeatedly said you were stupid (*Wound*). Every time you did not do something exactly as he wanted, he made the same comment about your intelligence. His words hurt and embarrassed you, particularly when they were spoken in front of your family. When frustrated, your dad would say you were witless, and when he did, your brother and sisters would laugh at you. Over time they even grew to call you

Wit, a nickname that people came to know you by more than your real name. And, after a while, since dad was seemingly smarter, you believed him. You accepted his judgment. And you concluded that because you were not as smart as others, you were less lovable and defective (*False Belief*).

Living with those false beliefs was far from easy. The thought that you were not as smart, lovable, and acceptable as your siblings brought significant emotional pain. You often felt sad, embarrassed, depressed, and filled with deep shame (*Emotional Upheaval*). Those are hard feelings to handle, so you started to kill the pain with food (*Dysfunctional Behavior*). You were not aware that you were eating because of emotional pain. But subconsciously you realized that chocolate candy, ice cream, donuts, and cake always made you feel better. It simply became a natural part of your day-to-day life.

Unfortunately, you are now an adult and you have a huge problem with your weight and, as a result, your health (*Life Situation*). Neither you nor your friends even consider that there is a link between your over eating and your father's hurtful words and attitude. Nor do they see that when you are stressed you eat more. But you do. In most areas of your life you are as "normal" as the next person. But there is a distortion of reality deep within that is causing you real problems.

What's the answer to this "imaginary" scenario? A person trapped in dysfunctional behaviors needs to meet Jesus in the wounds of the past and experience the healing of memories. I have seen it happen countless times, and have myself been freed by such encounters with the Lord. Through formational prayer, I have walked with people as they have re-entered a painful memory with Jesus, re-experiencing the painful past. I have watched as they, in the safety of his protective love, released the pent up emotional pain the past has caused. I was there as many, through the felt power of the Holy Spirit, renounced the lies that were spoken into them by others.

Filled with the presence of Christ, they were able to declare the truth, joyfully announcing that they were the children of God, salt of the earth, and chosen of the Most High. They spoke with boldness that they possessed the mind of Christ, are lavishly loved by the Father, and were fearfully and wonderfully made. I also have been present when many believers then repented of the sinful ways they had been using to kill emotional pain: sexual addictions, people pleasing, performance-based living, drug use, overeating, shopping, and a host of other dysfunctional behaviors. Since the root of wounding had been addressed, they were able to move forward in Christ toward the freedom of Spirit-directed living. The distorted life was traded for the abundant life promised by our Lord.

This process of deep healing is detailed in *Healing Care, Healing Prayer.* It will also be discussed in Chapter Six with specific reference to helping those who battle emotional disorders such as PTSD. The basic process is the same, whether a person is experiencing distortion or disorder. But with those who are battling disorder, the effects of the wounding are far more intense, and the process demands far more structure, as I will detail in Chapter Four and Chapter Five.

Disorder

In Chapter Two I shared what it is like to suddenly be capsized in life. It is an experience that goes far beyond distortion. It is in many ways disabling, accompanied by levels of fear and panic only understood by those who have experienced them. For me, it is tantamount to standing in water that is rising over my head and I am fighting to somehow get a breath and stay alive. I do anything possible to try to keep my nose above the water, and even the slightest life-splash threatens to undo me. Everything else about life seems unimportant, trumped by one desperate desire: to survive. And all of this terror and pain are coming from unprocessed pain caused by previous traumatic woundings. The cause and effect relationship between wounds, false beliefs, emotional upheaval, dysfunctional behavior, and life situation is essentially the same. However, the stress of the traumatic events and subsequent response are far more debilitating to the person because they have resulted in an emotional *disorder*.

In the previous description of distortion some aspect of the person's world leads to dysfunction, which means inappropriate behavior. With *disorder*, wounded people are incapable of functioning in some aspects of life. They are essentially disabled and unable to cope once the triggering occurs. Their emotions are on overload, they cannot think properly, they misinterpret events, and they quickly begin to withdraw and avoid situations. When not triggered, it may appear that they are not struggling anymore than someone living in distortion. But once a life-situation engages feelings of the past, the effect is taken to an entirely new level. They can be stuck there for hours, days, and even weeks. A life in *disorder* is lived with chronic anxiety and fear, with the person constantly watching to protect themselves from any sudden storms. But it never works because the cause is not the presence of a sudden storm. Being capsized is about living constantly in such deep emotional waters that even the most non-threatening life-splash can turn a calm day into a life-altering storm.

At the heart of the problem is the effect traumatic woundings can have on the human brain. I am not in the least way qualified to speak to all the intricacies of brain anatomy, function, and effect. But I can explain, in elementary terms, some of what happens when a person keeps re-experiencing the emotions of a past wounding. There is a place in the brain called the amygdala that enables a person to feel emotions. At birth it is fully developed, which is why even the smallest baby can have feelings about what is going on around them and express lots of emotion. Another part of the brain called the hippocampus that is not as developed at birth, but over time grows so that a person can process emotions, release the pent up energy, and essentially remember what happened without re-experiencing all the feelings that were originally experienced.

For people who struggle with a disorder like PTSD, an overload of powerful emotions has built up over the years and is essentially stuck in the amygdala. The feelings were never properly released and processed and passed on to the hippocampus so that it could do its job of bringing some definition and meaning to what happened. The feelings of these unprocessed traumatic events are all there, like flood waters held behind a weak levee. When something happens in life that may deserve a small emotional response, the amygdala kicks in and the person feels the full force of pent up, unprocessed, and unreleased emotions. They respond to a level 1 event with level 10 emotions. A life-splash that would normally be irritating at best causes feelings from the past to flood into the moment. And these feelings are so powerful that people respond with extreme fear or anger, or simply freeze, unable to function at all.

Like those with a distortion, people experiencing *disorder* are stuck in false beliefs, experience chronic unsettling feelings, and engage in dysfunctional behaviors. Most notably, they are often disabled by the sudden onslaught of unprocessed feelings from the past that make it almost impossible to function. Distortion is a significant problem, but *disorder* is a severe problem and causes many people to live in prisons of darkness and despair. Yet, Jesus came to set prisoners free, even those locked in dungeons of a traumatic past event. He is able and willing to enter the past with people and help them process the feelings keeping them in chains. And through his healing presence, Jesus can heal the human brain so that it can function the way he designed. It is the good news of the kingdom, a process that I will discuss later.

What follows in Chapter Four and Chapter Five is a description of the resources needed for the healing process to take place. The list I will share grew out of my own experience of being locked in a PTSD episode. If I had any hope of moving forward toward an encounter with Jesus in the pain of the past, these resources had to be within reach. I believe if you, like me, are on this difficult journey, you will find them just as important. If you are a caregiver, I admonish you not to start formational prayer until you have made a way for these resources to be in place.

Chapter Four

THE THINGS I NEED

People who struggle with the effects of traumatic wounding are highly hesitant to allow anyone into the pain of their past. They work hard to keep emotional turmoil at bay, and do not relish the thought of someone messing around in there. They are concerned that someone might touch something that will trigger an overwhelming flood of feelings. It takes a great deal of trust for traumatically wounded people even to put a toe into those deep waters. Even when they do, they will be constantly evaluating the sensitivity and insight the caregiver brings to the process. For most, the only reason they would even consider getting help is that life is becoming increasingly unbearable.

Addressing the effects of traumatic wounding is a process, not a moment in time. There is much to do before people begin to experience Jesus in the place of wounding. And there is work to be done after the encounter with Christ takes place. Receiving this type of care, or agreeing to walk with someone through the process, involves a commitment of time, energy, and trust. It demands a high level of engagement and, for the caregiver, an active willingness to provide the resources that will make the process effective. What follows is a description of those resources.

Safety

People who battle emotional disorders do not feel safe in life. I can not say that more emphatically or more simply. Traumatic events have conditioned the wounded to anticipate sudden disaster at any moment. Pathways have been formed in the brain and when something the least bit threatening occurs, flight, fight, or freeze responses automatically kick into gear. Even the shadow of a truck coming at the wounded can elicit panic and an instinctive desire to run. The unprocessed feelings of the wounding event are never far from the surface. Life is lived hyper-vigilant and anxious. Not only do most people who suffer PTSD feel unsafe with people, places, and things, they feel unsafe within their own skin. It seems as if their bodies are betraying them. They are attentive to every feeling, thought, and emotion they experience, anticipating that something bad might be just around the corner.

As mentioned earlier, most people who struggle work hard to keep some type of "life-raft" close at hand at all times. I lived many years assessing my environment, trying to find a way to save myself if necessary. In some cases I would try to keep "safe people" within reach, to help in case something happened. My wife or children or one or two of my closest friends could serve that role. If teaching or preaching, I would want them close. Safety could mean avoiding certain places, or having my Bible with me, or maybe checking to see just how far away from the hospital I was, in case of emergency. And, when I talk with others who struggle with the effects of deep wounding, it has been much the same.

I was predisposed to believe that I was unsafe. My earliest memory is one of sheer terror. I was about three or four years old when my grandfather took me for a ride one night when we were visiting. I can still remember getting into his tan car, with the dark brown velour seats. He drove out the driveway, past McConnahay's country store, and up the hill into the country. After a little while, he took the car down a dark, dirt lane and then parked it by a fence. I had been standing by him on the seat and he picked me up, put me in the back and told me to lie quietly on the floor until he returned. With that, my grandfather got out of the car, locked the doors behind him, and went off. I did not see the direction he went, but I could hear him walking away.

I was terrified. I wanted to scream, but was afraid if I did someone would come and hurt me. My heart was racing, and every movement and sound outside made me shiver in fright. I had never experienced such darkness, so thick that it felt like it was going to swallow me up. I waited and waited, and yet no grandfather. I had no idea where I was, feared that bad people were outside, and shook all over like a leaf in a wind storm. It was awful. But more than that, it was evil. After what seemed like an eternity, my grandfather returned, suddenly opening the door, seemingly out of breathe and in a hurry. He quickly started the car, drove out of the lane onto the road, and then told me to climb over the seat to the front. Nothing was said, except that we were now going back home and then to bed.

First, for anyone to do that to a child is far more than wrong; it is criminal. Worse, to then act like nothing happened and insist that I go to bed afterward made things even worse. An event like that can permanently affect a child's psyche, as it certainly did mine. For a long time I had no idea what happened that night. Some years later I brought it up to my parents, who initially said I was way too young to remember such an event. But when I described the car and details, they relented that it might have happened to me.

My grandfather died when I was four, so I had no way to ever find out more about it. For years all I knew was that it happened, that I was terrified, and that it was my earliest life memory. But just last fall, my dad shared the missing piece with me. My grandfather was a notorious womanizer, and the place I described was where he would go to meet secretly with women and have sex. Apparently, that was what was happening that night, and I was just the excuse to get him out of the house, away from my grandmother. He simply used me, and then manipulated the circumstance to keep me quiet. It is sickening to consider even now. If anyone, relative or not, tried to do anything remotely like that to my children or grandchildren, I'd have them jailed. For me, it was a tragic experience that helped birth the nightmare I have lived for many years.

Most people who suffer the effects of traumatic wounding have such memories, and like me they will not face the past unless they feel safe in the present. Safety does not mean the absence of all risk, but it does mean that an environment is created to eliminate all unnecessary risk. And safety begins with feeling safe with the caregivers. Wounded people want to know that they will be treated with care, compassion, and respect by their caregiver. They will respond best if caregivers display a welcoming presence, approach them with warmth, and are appropriately vulnerable. Caregivers who take the stance of wounded healers are far more likely to engender safety than those who are abrupt, clinical, and coldly objective. Personally, I would not allow a person like that to lead me across the street, let alone into my painful past, no matter how educated or qualified he or she might be. The wounded healer knows what it is like to be on the journey and will bring that experience into the process.

Safety is in part a matter of trust and trust will not come easily for most wounded people. That is especially true for those wounded by people who were in positions of authority. Even when their words say *yes*, deep within there is a lot of *no* until they sense that their caregivers have integrity. Certainly competence is part of feeling safe. I would not go to just anyone for help. I would want to know that the caregiver was a godly, Spirit-filled Christian. It would be important that the caregiver have a proven ability and anointing to walk the wounded through the formational prayer process. I would not necessarily look to find the caregiver's academic diploma somewhere on the wall. But I would try to look into their soul and find Jesus there.

I would also want to find out just how invested the caregiver was in the journey. It is essential that I know the caregiver's commitment to the Lord, to my healing, and to the entire process. I would not want to look up in the middle of it all and find that he or she was no longer there. And even more than being there, I would want to know that, all things considered, if things got tough the caregiver was experienced and confident in helping me walk through to freedom. And with all of that in place, I would likely feel safer but not completely at ease.

There is another critical aspect of safety. I mentioned earlier that most wounded people do not feel safe, even within their own skin. When I am helping a person experience Christ in a wounded past, I always spend time helping the person find a safe place within where he or she can meet Jesus. I do this through a basic prayer exercise that engages the Spirit-directed imagination of the wounded person. It is not pretending, which is unhelpful to the process. It is opening the imagination to the Holy Spirit so that he can help one picture in the mind's eye the reality of the Lord's love and care.

Communicating truth by creating word pictures is employed all through scripture. Isaiah said that God gathers the lambs in his arms and carries them close to his heart (Isaiah 40:11). The Psalmist talks about being covered by the wings of God and finding refuge under his feathers (Psalm 91:4). In both cases, the Lord was speaking metaphorically, creating a picture in the reader's mind so that he or she could better comprehend God's protective care. Creating a safe place within is a way that the Spirit communicates truth through a surrendered and sanctified imagination. When the Spirit does speak, the truth will always be consistent with the teachings of scripture, which is in itself the test for what one is seeing, sensing, and hearing during the exercise. The safe place exercise is as follows.

- *Sit quietly in a comfortable position.*

- *Take several deep breaths, letting them out slowly.*

- *Begin to whisper words of thanks and praise to the Lord.*

- *After a few moments, invite the Holy Spirit to take over your imagination.*

- *Ask the Spirit to create within your mind a safe place where you can meet the Lord. It may be an imaginary place or somewhere you have been before that is special, like a cabin, beach, or spot along a quiet stream.*

- *Rest there for as long as you like, enjoying all the surroundings. If you experience some dissonance or distraction, ask the Holy Spirit to take it away in the name of Jesus.*

- *When ready, invite the Lord to join you in that place. If that frightens you, ask him to come as the Lamb, or to simply allow you to feel his presence.*

- *Once there, notice the warmth of his love. Let it soak into your being. If you are allowing Christ to be there, notice his posture, eyes, and extended arms. Draw close to him if you desire.*

- *When ready, tell Jesus how you feel about him. Then ask how he feels about you. He may respond with words or maybe actions. Either way, experience his acceptance and delight.*

- *If you are ready to conclude the exercise, simply spend a few moments in thanks and praise.*

- *Take a few deep breaths, letting them out slowly.*

- *Amen*

This safe place exercise should be guided, especially at first, by the caregiver. He or she should watch to be sure that there is no interference from the evil one or distorted images that try to creep into the experience. That does occur at times and can be a particular problem for people who have had previous experiences in cults, ritualistic abuse, or new age mysticism. Some of those who have had exposure to such un-Christian practices have experienced distorted images of Jesus that are rooted in the demonic. This is evil and is designed to deceive people and distract them from the true Light of Christ. Caregivers should be careful to properly instruct people in the exercise and monitor what is happening so as to keep people centered in the Living Christ and not something distorted or demonic. New believers or those unfamiliar with the exercise would do best not to launch out alone. It is important for them to receive mentoring in the safe place exercise from caregivers, pastors, or other mature Christians.

For some people it takes time to develop this skill. Many believers, accustomed to a more cognitive expression of the Christian life, have never experienced the Lord in this way. The idea of giving the Lord access to their "creative imagination" will seem like a foreign concept. They will need encouragement and patient instruction in seeking the help of the Holy Spirit. They may find it helpful to include music, incense, or a candle as a way of opening the spiritual senses. And it is important that the wounded person practice this spiritual exercise every day. It will not only help him or her find within a place of peace with the Lord, it will, as discussed later, be the entrée into experiencing the Lord in the healing of past traumatic woundings.

Support

One of the most beautiful stories in all of scripture involves a paralyzed man and his group of friends (Mark 2:1-12). Jesus had returned home to Capernaum and, as usual, crowds of people gathered to hear him preach. The house was packed so people crowded at the door to listen. A group of men arrived carrying a paralyzed man on a mat. I have always wondered about the background to this account. Who were these men who brought a hurting friend to Jesus? Had they been lifelong pals, devoted to each other since childhood? Or maybe they had all worked together and one of them had been severely injured. Maybe the paralyzed man was a relative, and the group was made up of his brothers, cousins, and uncles. Whoever they were, they were obviously committed to the wounded man.

The house was full and the Lord was preaching. But these friends were determined that two things happen. They wanted their friend to get into the house and they wanted Jesus to heal him. Refused entry through the door, they went to the roof and began to dig. I cannot imagine their boldness and determination. It made no difference that they were destroying someone's property, exposing the inside to the winds and rain. They knew that could be fixed easily. But their friend's only chance at being repaired was in the hands of the One in the room below. And nothing was going to keep them from getting him to Jesus.

After opening a hole in the roof, the men lowered the paralytic to Jesus. The Bible says that Jesus "saw their faith" (Mark 2:5). When the broken man no longer believed, they believed for him. Their involvement, their compassion, their effort, their faith positioned the paralytic before the Lord for healing. And following an exchange with the teachers of the law, Jesus told him to get up, take the mat he had been lying on, and return home. He did get up and walk, and the people said, "We have never seen anything like this" (Mark 2:12). I know that the wonderful miracle in this story is the healing touch of Jesus. But part of the beauty of this account is the devotion of a group of men who were determined to see their friend set free.

This wonderful account can serve as a metaphor for what those paralyzed by traumatic wounding need. Their only hope is Jesus, and in most cases people are going to need help getting there. It will take incredible support from family, friends, and caregivers. And when broken people have little faith and no energy to move on, the faith and prayer of those who are close will matter most. They must be willing to do whatever is necessary, even if it means doing what may not be proper or popular. They must be that committed, that determined, that involved in the process of healing.

I have a deep concern when people seek to experience deep healing and the only one involved is their counselor. No matter how devoted the caregiver may be, a one-on-one relationship is simply not enough. There must be others who support the process. The hurting person must be connected to other people in the body of Christ. Even if they do not know the details of what is taking place with the counselor, their prayers, acceptance, and love provide strength for the journey. They provide a connection to Christ and a net of safety when things get tough. The caregiver must be equally committed to this, encouraging involvement in the community of Christ. When possible the caregiver should find ways to initiate networks of support for the hurting person.

Many people, myself included, are very hesitant to talk with people about what is going on inside. If anything, most of us withdraw when things are tough rather than seek the support of others. This is often driven by the fear that people will think we are weak, or messed up, or even crazy. And indeed there are people who would feel exactly like that about the problems faced by those who have experienced traumatic woundings. And those people should be avoided at all costs.

But God has designed Christians to be connected as brothers and sisters in Christ. It is the way he ordered the nation of Israel, with every person in a family, every family part of a clan, every clan part of a tribe, and every tribe part of the nation of Israel, and Israel part of the family of God. He meant for them to be connected. Jesus was connected to people, from his special three—Peter, James, and John—to the twelve, to the seventy, to the 120 and so forth. As it says in Genesis, being alone is not good (Genesis 2:18).

I am on a journey of healing that I cannot make alone. It is just that simple. I must have the resource of friends and family to make it through to freedom in Christ. Gratefully, I do have a network of support and those brothers and sisters have proven faithful, even when I am hard to handle. They are the hands and feet of Jesus to me, and I need them desperately. I am convinced that responsible caregivers must be sure that this support is provided for the people under their care. And a person seeking freedom from the effects of past traumatic wounding should not move forward until support is in place.

Permission Seeking and Invitation

I had been teaching the doctoral students every day for a week and was feeling a bit tired. Instead of standing to teach, I chose to sit on a stool and lecture. As I did, one of the students asked if I was tired, and I said yes, but I would be fine. With that, the student stood and said, "Let's all surround Dr. Wardle, lay hands on him and pray." I love these students deeply, and they are some of my favorite people on earth. Yet as they arose and started to move forward, I stopped them and said, "I deeply appreciate your willingness to pray for me, but I need you to ask permission before you come up here and lay hands on me."

I could tell that my statement brought them up short, but I did not regret saying it. I experienced immediate discomfort when the student determined to gather his classmates and move into my space. Even though his intentions were good, his approach was inappropriate and I was not going to simply bear up silently. I needed them to respect my boundaries: I had every right to determine if I wanted them to touch me, as does every person.

I expect people to seek my permission before they draw into what I deem to be an intimate moment with me. It is not that I want to keep everyone out or at a distance. I like being touched, enjoy receiving prayer, and appreciate experiencing genuine connection. But those are all intimate actions and thus require permission. I get to determine who, when, and how a person enters my space. Some, like members of my family and close friends, have essentially an open invitation. But beyond that, I expect people to ask.

Many people who have experienced traumatic wounding did so at the hands of those who did not respect their boundaries. They were touched in ways that were wrong and harmful. Some were beaten as children, grabbed violently, or sexually abused. Others were disrespected in less violent, yet harmful ways. I know many people who were not permitted to have any rights or space of their own. A person once told me that when she was living at home her father would consistently walk in on her when she was in the bathroom or enter her bedroom at will. If she complained about such intrusions, he berated her, shouting that it was his house, she was his daughter, and he would do what he wanted. She was humiliated by his behavior but powerless to do anything about it. Her mother's unwillingness to deal with the matter on her behalf was equally as wounding.

Thoughtful caregivers recognize the importance of seeking permission, particularly given the sensitive nature of traumatic woundings. It will be important that caregivers ask permission to pray, lay hands, close a door, draw near, anoint with oil, bless with holy water, and invite someone else into a session. These are intimate acts and the person must have the opportunity to say yes or no. And regardless of the answer, the response must be honored.

Caregivers have the right to ask why the wounded person said no. And it is important that the individual talk about why, sharing the thoughts and feelings that drove the response. The caregiver may even want to explain further what is behind the request, and ask the person to reconsider. But in the end, the response must be honored. By doing so, the individual will feel respect, become a more active part of the process, and invariably appreciate and trust the caregiver all the more.

Invitation is also an important resource for the process of deep healing. Our neighbors had a most contentious relationship. I do not remember many kind words shared between them in all the years they were alive. They told each other what to do, even down to the minutest activity of life. It was not, "please pass the ketchup," spoken with manners. One would shout across the table, "Give me the ketchup." To which the other would either respond, "Get it yourself," or "Here!" Their words were harsh, and as a child I felt uncomfortable when they spoke to each other like that. It frightened me because they seemed so angry. Granted, that is not a life altering wound. But it did create dis-ease for me in an already crazy-making world.

Many people, however, feel that the directives and commands coming from aggressive people are aimed directly at them. My friend Jimmy had a father who told him to do something...one time. If he had to repeat himself, Jimmy was going to get hit. He knew that there was an unspoken phrase that followed every command: "or else." The actual "or else" was swift and painful, and it did not take Jimmy long to recognize that for his own protection, he'd better jump. But Jimmy grew to despise his father and was constantly battling stomach problems. He grew up to be a very angry man and an alcoholic. As a child Jimmy had a tremendous sense of humor and a tender heart. But all that most people see of Jimmy today is a broken person struggling to keep from capsizing.

A caregiver must invite, not command. There is a world of difference between, "Sit here" and "Would you like to sit here?" During a session a caregiver may sense that a person is experiencing some anxiety. But there is a real difference between, "Go to your safe place now," and "Would you like to go to your safe place?" When moving through the formational prayer process, it is far better for the caregiver to ask, "Would you like to move on or do you want to stay were you are right now?" as opposed to simply telling a person to move to the next step in the process. These are no small matters, for they impact the way a wounded person feels about the caregiver and the experience of deep healing. The caregiver should respect space as well as invite participation. Both are critically important to me, and I believe just as valuable to any wounded person seeking help along the path.

Opening of the Senses

Over the years of my struggle with PTSD I tried increasingly to get away from my feelings and live life in my head. The feelings inside were strong and unpredictable and I simply did not trust them. Chronic anxiety and fear made feelings my enemy, so I did my best to push them back. I worked to approach life more stoically, embracing the false belief that emotions can't be trusted. And there were more than a few reinforcements for that idea. Growing up in a home where feelings were not processed and tears discouraged rather than valued was one. And, given that most educational systems were driven by concepts shaped by the Enlightenment, school was a place where right thinking was prioritized over expressing emotion. The "thinking kids" were rewarded and the "feeling kids" often ridiculed.

My close friends once commented on how criticism or loss appeared not to bother me. The operative phrase is of course "appeared not to" because all the while I was working to keep myself from exploding inside. I once went so far as to tell several student pastors that it was important to develop a "poker face" so that people would not be able to know how you were really feeling. I said, "You need to get to the place where a person can be saying hurtful things about you and you do not even flinch." Of course this was horrible advice, shaped by wounding, not good judgment. It was not only a formula for emotional dishonesty, it lead to bottling up unprocessed feelings.

The irony in my attempt to distance from negative feelings in order to protect from pain was that it actually had the opposite effect on me. It kept me from experiencing good feelings and positive emotions, all the while strengthening the ever present fear and anxiety. It made things worse, not better. And because of this, and all the years of struggle, my brain was programmed to go quickly to bad feelings when something negative happened. It was difficult for me to experience good feelings. It was as if that part of my brain was less developed.

Anne Halley is a dear friend and one of the most gifted caregivers I know. She is particularly skilled at helping adults who were traumatically wounded as children and individuals who, like me, battle PTSD. Thankfully, I have been able to depend on Anne for help. One of the first things Anne did was encourage me to engage in more right brain activities. The basic theory behind right and left hemisphere brain function is quite interesting. It seems that the left hemisphere is the part of the brain that enables a person to engage in critical thinking, logical analysis, information gathering, and the like. It helps a person function logically, rationally, and objectively. When I said earlier that I was working to live "in my head," that is essentially what I meant. I was primarily engaging in left brain activities, seeking to gain knowledge, figure things out, and develop strategies for daily life.

The right hemisphere is the part of the brain that enables one to be intuitive and more subjective. It prioritizes aesthetics, feelings, and senses. Human imagination and creativity in the arts emanate from the "right brain." For many people who are locked in unprocessed memories of the past, the wonderful, creative potential of this part of the brain is untapped and undeveloped. However, it holds great powers for healing emotions. So a strategy must be initiated to access that power through the opening of the senses.

Anne assigned me right hemisphere activities and suggested that I spend some time each day using that part of my brain. She insisted that it would affect the process of recovery and the healing of traumatic wounds. Over the past few years I started to play the guitar again, took art lessons, and did some carving in wood. She also encouraged me to listen to music, burn incense when praying, and use a variety of symbols and icons as windows to experiential encounters with the Lord. She incorporated these into sessions of formational prayer. At times Anne has invited me to wrap myself in a soft blanket while receiving prayer. Admittedly I had to push through some initial resistance. But the benefits of opening the senses have been amazing. I find that these activities give rise to many positive feelings and bring me peace. And they provide an inner resource for the healing journey that I did not previously have.

Paying more attention to the five senses opens a person to a part of the internal world that holds restorative qualities. I have slowed down in order to pay far more attention to the beauty that surrounds me. I have begun to take photos of flowers, wildlife, and landscapes. I am noticing for the first time that there is a wonder and magic to creation that is absolutely stunning. I take time to sit in the sun and notice how it feels warming my skin. I try to pay attention to how the sand feels on my feet, how the gentle breeze caresses my cheek, and how marvelous it is to watch a summer sunset.

I have slowly peeled an orange, allowing myself to enjoy the feel of the skin in my hands. I have breathed deeply to catch the matchless fragrance that filled my nostrils. Unlike the past, I tend to eat an orange slowly, enjoying the sweet taste of the juice contained in every section. I pay attention to my feelings, as I am often filled with pleasure and delight in such a simple act. I can not help but feel grateful to God for the rich gift of an orange.

In the past I would have dismissed all this as "touchy feely" musings that count for little in life. How terribly wrong I was! I had cut myself off from a critical source of restoration and empowerment. Thankfully, a part of me long asleep is coming to life. And this "opening of the senses" is contributing to the healing I have so desperately needed. People who are locked in emotional disorders need the resource that the senses provide. They must be encouraged to step into the type of activities discussed here. It will most likely be difficult and not come naturally. But the responsible caregiver must persist, assigning sensate-based exercises to those they help. It is a resource of healing that the wounded will draw from all along the path to freedom.

Patience and Encouragement

Well over a decade ago Tommy and Jeannie Hignell invited Cheryl and me to join them for a weekend at Lake Almanor in Northern California. He knew that I was having a tough time and believed that a few days at his mountain cabin would be good for me. Tommy had become a dear friend over the years and was deeply concerned about my health. He was a physician and had already walked with me through some nightmarish times, which he always did with grace and generosity. I can look back and see several occasions where the only thing that kept me going was Tommy's encouragement. And what happened that weekend was a perfect example.

Late on Saturday afternoon, Tommy and I went to the dock and took off for a long ride on his wave runner. He liked to run it hard and fast and make as many waves as possible. We were far out into the lake when we were thrown from the wave runner while making a hairpin turn. It was great fun and we both laughed as we swam toward the stalled watercraft. I love the water and have had several boats over the years. This type of adventure was right up my alley—or at least so I thought.

Tommy and I fought to get back up on the wave runner, and he turned the key to start the motor. Nothing. The motor would not turn over. He tried everything, but somehow we had stalled the engine and it would not fire. I began to notice that I was experiencing some anxiety. But I pressed past it in order to help however I could. As it began to grow dark Tommy said, "We are going to have to swim this thing to shore."

That should have been no big deal. I love swimming and besides we were both wearing life vests. But as we slipped back into the water I got triggered big time. I went into emotional overload and within seconds I was locked into a PTSD encounter that had me by the throat. I was fighting back panic, having trouble breathing, and my heart was racing out of control. My thoughts became irrational, which made things all the worse. I was afraid I was going to die out there in the middle of the lake, if not by drowning, by heart attack! I had to say something to Tommy. So I simply turned to him and said, "I am in trouble."

Tommy saw the panic in my face and immediately started to patiently encourage me. He was calm, assuring me that he was right there and would not leave my side. He repeatedly told me that I could do this, and that he would help me. I was not only experiencing fear, but also shame and anger. I kept saying, "I am sorry, Tommy. Really, I am so sorry this happened. I so wish I were not like this. This is so embarrassing." Tommy lovingly said, "Its okay, really. It's what friends do for friends."

As we swam on across the lake, Tommy would check in with me. "How are you doing? Do you feel okay? You are really doing great. Frankly, I am proud of you." He never for a moment displayed ridicule or frustration. He was gentle and loving the entire time. Once we made the long swim to shore, he celebrated what I had done as though I had just crossed the English Channel. Back in the cabin, he continued to help me regain control. He spent time with me in prayer and helped me find some "solid ground" on which to stand. I am forever grateful to Tommy, and know I could not have made it without him.

I choose to be vulnerable about this experience, as terrible and humiliating as it was, because it illustrates how essential the resources of encouragement and patience are to those who have been affected by traumatic wounding. Anyone who has the courage to commit to the process of deep healing will need constant doses of both. I am honest about the healing of memories and tell people that it will get worse before it gets better. And it is all the tougher because some of the best opportunities for healing happen when a person has been triggered and is in the midst of an emotional episode.

Most wounded people want to run away from such times, not into them. Yet Jesus waits to meet them in the darkness. People seeking healing must be encouraged to press on with his help. And the resources of encouragement and patience are best distributed by a caregiver who, like Tommy, is constant in love, strong in faith, and tireless in service to a brother or sister in need.

> Let us hold unswervingly to the hope we profess, for he who promised is faithful. And let us consider how we may spur one another on toward love and good deeds...let us encourage one another all the more.... (Hebrews 10: 23-25)

Chapter Five

MORE THINGS I NEED

Caregivers would do well to view themselves as guides and outfitters for people who are setting forth on an arduous journey. In this case the people are men, women, and children who are living with the effects of traumatic wounding. The journey is into painful places of the past where Jesus waits to meet and free them. And the caregiver is there to provide support, point the way, and insure that those making the journey have the resources they need to see it through to the end. While the people making this journey must do what they can to anticipate their needs, they will invariably require items they did not anticipate. It is the caregiver's responsibility to provide help so the wounded can access what is necessary. Seven such resources—safety, support, permission seeking, invitation, opening the senses, patience, and encouragement—have already been addressed in the previous chapter. This chapter discusses six more resources so that both care-givers and those seeking freedom can better prepare for the journey.

Time and Space

Jesus had spent the Sabbath in Capernaum. The day began with Jesus teaching in the synagogue where, at one point, he freed a man from an evil spirit. After teaching he went to the home of Simon and Andrew, and there he healed Peter's mother of a fever that had confined her to bed. That evening the whole town gathered together and took all the sick and demonized people to the Lord. And the scripture says that Jesus healed them of many different diseases and drove away the evil spirits that inflicted many (Mark 1:21-37). This narrative is exciting because of the many healings and miracles Jesus performed. But what happened next is, to me, equally as amazing.

Mark records that very early the next morning Jesus went off to a solitary place and prayed (Mark 1:35-39). At some point his followers, who had been searching for him, arrived and told Jesus that people were looking for him. Jesus responds by telling them that they must leave Capernaum because he had to go preach in other towns. He was not going to be driven by the urgencies of the moment, or by any agenda other than God's. That even included such critical matters as healing and deliverance. Through prayer Jesus was able to refocus on the mission God had given him, and move on to fulfill that calling. Jesus had clear and balanced priorities and they determined how he invested his life on earth.

It does not take supernatural discernment to see that people today are driven, living hectic lives with unbalanced priorities. Lives are being spent at full speed traveling down a dead end street. People are trapped in the barrenness of busyness as they invest more of themselves in that which takes, and seldom gives. And many people are being hurt as a result. Children, spouses, health, friends, and spiritual well being are being sacrificed. A pastor friend of mine described it well when he said, "Some thing or some one other than me is controlling my time, and I am being lost in the process."

With that said, it must be clearly understood that the journey to freedom in Christ demands a serious time commitment. It is not like visiting the dentist and having a tooth filled in a single visit. It will involve formational prayer, with various assignments required between sessions. Working through the effects of traumatic woundings is life changing, but not accomplished quickly. The person wanting to take that journey cannot simply add it to an already over-committed schedule. It requires some serious subtracting if there is any hope of experiencing deep transformation.

Yes, Christ can heal a person in an instant. However, formational prayer is as much about the journey as it is the destination. And the journey will most likely take some time. It will demand serious reprioritizing. It is true that God is lavish in pouring out his grace upon the weak. But that grace does not come cheap. It involves deep commitment. And caregivers must also recognize that helping a person along this path will not happen without spiritual preparation, availability, and steady commitment. It will involve a significant amount of time.

It is almost frightening how driven we are in this society. And many people feel guilty when they take time for themselves, as though they are doing something wrong. I experienced those feelings even when I was debilitated and in the hospital. My doctor said that I needed extended rest and should take care of myself, and somehow I felt badly about that. But caring for oneself is part of faithful stewardship. And the wounded and weary must make room for self-care and deep healing. May those wounded by the effects of traumatic events hear Jesus invite them, as he did his weary followers long ago, to come apart and be with him and finally experience rest (Mark 6:31).

There are more than a few people in my world and I have some significant responsibilities. There are many expectations placed upon me, and some are rather important. Professionally I have deadlines to meet, papers to grade, dissertations to review, events to organize,

and people to help. My wife desires my involvement, my children my support, and my grandchildren my attention. Normally, I am happy to serve and experience the presence of Jesus as I do. But since saying yes to my own healing journey, I have needed these same people to give me space. For a season I have not been able to be as available as I have been in the past. I have not been "there" as much as normal because I have been somewhere else. I have been in my pain-filled past with Jesus.

In my professional life few people know why I am not as accessible as before. My assistant handles the questions and life goes on just fine. But in my personal life I have been upfront about what is happening and the need for grace and understanding. My wife, children, and close friends know all about my struggle and the healing journey I am on, and invariably they have responded with only the greatest support. I have described what I need and, frankly, they have gone far beyond that to provide space for me to fully engage in the process. Whether it is time away in retreat, or evenings receiving prayer, or simply time to reflect, they understand and say yes. That space is an invaluable resource for this season of healing.

People wanting to take this journey will need space. They will need space to struggle, and reflect, and experience Jesus, and heal. They may need to take walks alone, or meet with their caregivers more than once a week for formational prayer. They might need to set several days aside for a healing retreat. And they may need to say no to others in order to say yes to the Lord. The people closest to them will probably need to know why. That is where the caregiver can help by providing a strategy for sharing appropriately and asking for grace. But however it looks, walking into the past with Jesus involves both time and space, and most likely a great deal of both at least for a season. These two resources are not optional. They are essential to the entire healing process.

Explanation and Structure

For a person who has been deeply wounded by a traumatic event, not knowing what is coming next often produces anxiety. Moving into the unknown is not always an adventure, and that is especially true if it holds the potential of triggering a sudden, emotional flood. The hyper-vigilance mentioned previously keeps a wounded person ever watchful and wondering. The questions of the day are usually "What's next?" "What was that?" "How bad is this going to get?" "How long is it going to last?" And the answer, "Just relax, everything will be fine," seldom helps.

I well remember standing outside the entrance to the psychiatric hospital already convinced that my world had fallen apart. I had been battling for months and I wondered if I would ever pick up the pieces of my shattered life and put them together again. And while I knew I needed help, the challenge to walk through those glass entrance doors was terrifying. Rather than being relieved that I was there, I was overwhelmed with anxiety and fear. And in no small part, it was because I had no idea what was going to happen behind those locked doors. I felt out of control and saw neither guard rails nor roads signs to help me navigate through the experience.

I am sure that every person who saw me enter those doors knew I was terrified. It was written all over my face. But the staff was initially matter of fact with me. They had me fill out admission forms, and then instructed me to empty my suitcase for inspection. They then took all personal items like soap, razors, combs, etc., and placed them in a container to be kept at the front. My blood pressure was checked, which had to be off the charts, and then I was taken to my room and left to unpack. When the staff person left the room I sat down on my bed and cried. I felt alone, confused, and clueless as to what was coming next.

I am thankful that later in the day I was able to meet with someone and get enough answers to keep me from bolting out the doors.
And in time I came to love the people there and appreciate the depth
of care they provided. But my experience those first hours was a
nightmare. And it could have easily been different if someone had
simply explained a few things and put some structure on what was
going to happen in the upcoming days. The one good result of that
experience is that it has left me with an unwavering commitment
to provide the people I help with a structured experience from the
very first moment we meet. I want them to have a description of the
"guard rails" in place, "road signs" to keep them on course, and as
many "mile markers" as possible to show progress along the way.

I am well aware that the path through the dark night is not easily
mapped. There will be many unknown challenges along the way, and
the topography of each person's journey is different. But caregivers
owe it to people to provide some needed explanation and structure.
They should try to eliminate as much anxiety and fear as possible.
That begins from the first moment of contact, when the caregiver
meets the person with a welcoming attitude. The caregiver must
show immediate attention to the wounded person and communicate
care, compassion, and confidence in every way possible. And right
from the start, the caregiver must make it clear that every question
is important and encouraged. Genuine interest in the apprehensions
and concerns of a wounded person go a long way toward relieving
tension. It builds the caregiver's credibility as well.

I have found it very helpful to describe early on what will take
place in the sessions. I share my expectations for the weekly assignments and talk about why they are important to the process. I spend
time reinforcing my dependence on the Lord and faith in his presence
throughout the process. I assure the person that I will spend time
preparing for each session. And I tell them that I will pray regularly
for them and for their journey to transformation and healing. Most

importantly, I assure them that I want to hear their complete story that caused them to seek help.

In Chapter Three I shared the basic cause and effect relationship between wounds, false beliefs, emotional upheaval, dysfunctional behaviors and the impact each has on a person's life situation. I have those concepts made into a small chart and take time to explain them in one of the initial sessions with people. I encourage caregivers to do the same.

Life Situation

Dysfunctional Behavior

Emotional Upheaval

False Beliefs

Wounds

It is good to begin by talking about *wounds,* going over the basic typology of traumatic wounding. It is important to explain how traumatic woundings can affect a person and why some people are more impacted than others. The caregiver should encourage the person to ask as many questions as needed. The caregiver should go on to say some things about *false beliefs* and how they result from wounds. It may be helpful to share an anecdote that illustrates how such lies develop and the toll they take on people's lives. Most people quickly grasp the concept and begin to reflect on possible false beliefs they may battle.

People affected by traumatic wounding understand the power of *emotional upheaval.* However, it can be helpful to discuss how unprocessed feelings of the past can build up and then come flooding in when a person is triggered. I know how important it was for me to learn that the overwhelming flood of emotions that would suddenly capsize me were coming from wounds I received in childhood.

It enabled me to better understand the nature of the disorder and encouraged me to say yes to the healing process.

The caregiver would do well to explain the nature of *dysfunctional behaviors* and why people engage in them. I find it helpful to discuss how dysfunctional behaviors are often used as a means of killing the pain of past woundings. But it is also important to talk about how wounded people use dysfunctional behaviors to try to keep themselves safe. Invariably, this little bit of explanation initiates a great deal of thought about how the person kills pain and works to keep safe. The caregiver should also talk about the concept of *life situation*: how the context of day-to-day life becomes the place where dysfunctional behaviors occur, and that it is where most emotional upheaval is triggered. Caregivers may find the imaginary story about "Wit," found in Chapter Three as a helpful way to illustrate the relationship between each of the elements in this model.

All throughout the journey to healing the caregiver should explain each part of the process. That includes the steps to the formational prayer process yet to be discussed in Chapter Six. The wounded person should be clear about what is expected of them. At any time along the way the person should either have or be able to receive enough information to know where they are in the process, how far they have come, and what yet lies ahead. Granted, there will be many unknowns. And since the healing process is guided by the ministry of the Holy Spirit, there can never be a detailed instruction manual. Even so, helping a wounded person understand and see the basic structure of care will go a long way toward reducing unnecessary fear and anxiety.

Spiritual Exercises

I must confess that as a Protestant Christian, the concept of spiritual exercises was foreign to me. I mistakenly believed that such activities were part of an unhealthy mysticism void of balance and spiritual depth. But when the dark night of the soul descended and all my normal ways of responding to life failed, the writings of the Christian mystics helped me find my way home again. Along the way I discovered several spiritual exercises that quietly, yet power-fully, brought understanding and life back into my lost and weary soul. Handling the difficulties of an emotional disorder demanded that I deepen my relationship with Christ. In desperation I willingly embraced vehicles of his grace that I might not have previously con-sidered. I have never been the same, and the practices of the saints have become special vehicles of grace.

There are many spiritual exercises that hold potential for meet-ing the Lord and developing a greater openness to the ministry of the Holy Spirit. And whether by choice or by assignment from a caregiver, an individual who has been wounded by traumatic events should regularly practice some of them. They will help the person develop a deeper capacity for the presence of Christ that is essential to the healing of memories and release from the effects of traumatic wounds. I am including here a brief discussion of five exercises: simple prayer, breath prayer, scripture, solitude, and sacrament.

Simple Prayer

Most people find prayer intimidating. They mistakenly think that to be acceptable before the Lord prayers must be said in just the right way, with just the right words. But Jesus is not impressed with long rambling prayers that have the appearance of spiritual maturity, but are in fact self-serving and empty (Matthew 6: 5-13). He encouraged his followers to practice more simple forms of prayer.

For centuries believers all over the world have used the Jesus Prayer as a way of making their requests known to the Lord. The Jesus Prayer comes from the cry of a blind beggar who was at the side of the road calling out for Jesus to help him (Luke 18:35-43).

Upon discovering that the Lord was near, the blind beggar called out, "Jesus, Son of David, have mercy on me." People told him to be quiet, but he just shouted all the more, "Jesus, Son of David, have mercy on me!" The Lord was deeply moved by the man, complimented him on his faith, and healed him of blindness.

To people struggling with the effects of traumatic wounding, the words, "Jesus, Son of David, have mercy on me," are packed with meaning. All the requests of the broken are contained in those eight words. The caregiver should prayerfully introduce the Jesus Prayer to those they serve. I personally instruct individuals to picture every prayer need they have entering those eight words. By doing so, they can lift all their concerns before the Lord in one simple prayer. Broken people should pray the Jesus Prayer many times a day, allowing it to draw them toward the One who hears, who cares, and who will answer their cry.

Breath Prayer

The spiritual exercise called breath prayer was developed by Ron DelBene, and discussed in his book *The Breath of Life: A Simple Way to Pray.* The breath prayer constitutes a person's deepest heart cry. It is normally only a short phrase or sentence that expresses an individual's spiritual hunger. When prayed, it opens the heart to a new attentiveness and awareness of the Father's love and desire to touch a person at the point of their greatest need. Discovering one's breath prayer occurs through a simple visualization exercise.

A person is to sit quietly before the Lord, opening herself to the presence of the Holy Spirit. She is then to imagine the Lord standing with arms extended, calling the person by name and asking her, "(Name), what do you most want from me?" With that the broken person allows the answer to come from the deepest place within the heart. That cry, contained in a few words, becomes a breath prayer. It can be prayed as often as the person desires, a constant reminder of the individual's most earnest desire. For the wounded, this prayer can become the "prayer without ceasing" that Paul wrote about in First Thessalonians (1 Thessalonians 5:17).

Scripture

There is life and nourishment in the Word of God. It is alive with the Spirit and contains wonderful truths that can sustain people through even the darkest times. It is particularly important that those wounded by traumatic events spend time reading and meditating on Scripture. Caregivers should help people read the Bible in ways that enable them to encounter the power of the living Word. There are many valuable approaches to encountering the Lord in scripture and a personal favorite is known as the *Lectio Divina*.

Lectio Divina is an ancient approach to scripture that has been widely practiced in the church. It involves a very slow reading of the Word in connection with a form of contemplative prayer. *Lectio Divina* has four movements. First, a person reads a short passage of scripture, allowing God to speak through the text. That is called the *lectio* or listening phase. Next, the reader thinks about the implications of the scripture as it relates to what God spoke to the person's heart. This is called *meditatio or* meditation.

Next the reader moves into a form of prayer that is far more dialogue than monologue. The reader begins a loving, intimate conversation with the Father, talking with God about what the text holds for her personally. The reader wants the Spirit to take the truth into the deepest place within her heart. This phase is known as *oratio* or prayer. Finally, the reader rests quietly before God, surrendering to the Holy Spirit as he brings deep change and transformation. This phase is known as *contemplation*. The caregiver might want to select brief passages for the person that relate to the journey to freedom in Christ. I often choose specific passages from Ephesians that highlight the believer's standing and position as children of God. I ask the person I am serving to practice the *lectio* model through these texts, asking the Holy Spirit to plant the truth of God's Word deep within their hearts.

Solitude

John Michael Talbot has written a powerful book about Saint Francis entitled, *The Lessons of Saint Francis: How to Bring Simplicity and Spirituality into Your Daily Life.* In it he writes, "By practicing the discipline of solitude, we are creating a space in our lives where God can be with us. And over time, as that space grows, so can our relationship with the living God."[7] Most people have made very little space for God, filling their lives with people and activities, in a desperate effort to keep distance from their own brokenness. But the saints of the past, like Francis, believed that solitude was the only way to confront those personal demons.

Solitude is much different than isolation. Isolation is about running away, withdrawing in an effort to hide and create a semblance of what they think is safety. Solitude on the other hand, is a running toward God in order to face the truth and confront it in the power of Christ. Many people do not know what to do in solitude, and wonder if it will be boring, a waste of time, or worse, an invitation to personal uneasiness. The caregiver should help the person confront such fears, and move into solitude seeking an encounter with the Lord. Using scripture, the safe place exercise, simple prayer, breath prayer and other spiritual exercises while in solitude can position a broken person for a visitation of the Father of light and love.

The Eucharist

"On the night Jesus was betrayed, he took bread and broke it, saying, 'This is my body given for you; do this in remembrance of me.' Later in much the same way he took the cup and said, 'This cup is the new covenant in my blood, which is poured out for you'" (Luke 22: 7-22). Since that Passover night, Christians have gathered to celebrate the

Eucharist. Partaking of the Lord's Supper is one of the most important moments in the life of Christians.

Celebrating the Eucharist can position a wounded person for a healing encounter with the Lord. The caregiver should consider incorporating this sacrament into the time spent with broken people. It is a wonderful act of covenant love between Christians and Jesus. I would encourage the caregiver to have elements available for use in sessions. In some traditions consecrating the elements can only be done by the ordained clergy. In that case, I encourage the caregiver to have pastors pray over the elements before distributing them. However accomplished, the spiritual exercise of sacrament is one of the most important ways broken people are positioned for the transforming touch of Christ.

The symbols of crushed wheat and squeezed grapes are powerful to the wounded and bruised. They remind people that Jesus allowed his body to be broken and his blood to be shed so that they can be transformed. His wounds have become for them the channel of God's healing touch. Jesus is, as Henri Nouwen often said, the Wounded Healer. The Eucharist, though, is much more than a symbol. It is a celebration of Jesus with Jesus present. He is there to commune with his people and nourish their souls and body with his everlasting life. I tell people who are seeking the healing touch of Christ to never walk to the table of the Lord. Run!

Episodic Encounters with God

Years ago a Jesuit priest named Jean-Pierre de Caussade was assigned the responsibility of serving as spiritual guide for a group of nuns. Much of his guidance is contained in the book, *The Sacrament of the Present Moment.* There he writes:

> You are seeking God, dear sister, and he is everywhere. Everything proclaims him to you, everything reveals him to you, everything brings him to you. He is by your side, over you, around you, within you...you seek perfection and it lies in everything that happens to you—your suffering, your actions, your impulses are the mysteries under which God reveals himself to you.[8]

The importance of de Caussade's point must not be lost to the broken people needing help or to the caregivers who serve them.

God is not simply to be learned about in life. He is to be experienced. He waits in every moment to be encountered by those who seek him. He longs to fill people's hearts with indescribable love, overwhelm them with incomparable peace, and flood their minds with unspeakable joy. Yes, he desires to meet people in the memories of the painful past. But before that can happen, wounded people must discover God in the sacrament of the present moment. He is there, ready to be experienced by the people he unconditionally loves.

In the poem "Aurora Leigh," Elizabeth Barrett Browning wrote, "Earth's crammed with heaven, every common bush afire with God; but only he who sees takes off his shoes; the rest sit round it and pick blackberries." All of creation is alive with the presence of God, yet most people miss him. They complain that God is distant and silent. But the real problem lies with people. They do not have "eyes that see and ears that hear." They have not developed their spiritual senses and have difficulty seeing and sensing the movement of the Lord in life.

Earlier I addressed the importance of developing the "right brain" in order to open the senses. It is the right brain that enables a person to fall in love, connect emotionally with people, sense what others are feeling, imagine wonderful things, delight in a sunrise, enjoy the taste of an orange...and experience God in every moment of every day.

While the left brain enables a person to understand the teachings of scripture, increase knowledge of theology, and think great thoughts about God, it does not give a person an experiential encounter with him. That comes from the opening of right brain sensitivities. It happens when a person positions himself to encounter God in the moments of life, whether that moment be during worship in a church, or when meditating on a scripture, or watching the sunset over a distant hill.

Once again, the difficulty for people who have been affected by traumatic events is that they have in many ways shut themselves off from their feelings. They want to keep as far away from them as possible. It is not that they want to disconnect from all feelings. Theoretically they want distance from only the bad feelings. But in reality it does not work out that way. People who "live in their head" end up staying away from the good feelings as well. They "disconnect" and then cannot access all the wonderful moments of life and experiences of the presence of God accessed through the senses. The only time they "feel" is when triggered and all the unprocessed emotions of the past come flooding into their lives.

God desires that people experience him episodically, through right brain sensitivities. This term episodic is very important to the work of deep healing though formational prayer. I want to develop the concept here as it relates to experiencing God in the wonderful moments of life. In the next chapter will discuss the same concept, only there it will relate to experiencing Christ in the traumatic moments of the past. Practicing the episodic encounter as discussed here, in the sacrament of the present moment, lays the spiritual foundation for encountering the Lord episodically in the healing of traumatic woundings of the past through formational prayer.

Daniel Schacter wrote a book called *Searching for Memory*. He is a behavioral scientist from Harvard and specializes in memory function within the human brain. He has developed a concept of memory that has greatly helped my understanding of the healing of traumatic woundings. Schacter says that we have three basic types of memory: procedural memory, semantic memory, and episodic memory.[9]

Procedural memory is comprised of those activities that we are able to do automatically. While initially we had to think about what it took to do a certain "procedure," a time comes when we are able to remember how to do it without consciously thinking about all that it involves. It becomes part of a larger category of memory called instinctive memory. Take writing, for example. When I first began to write I had to think about each step. I tried to remember the correct way to hold a pencil, make the shapes of the alphabet, move my hand across the paper from left to right, and so forth. But in time all that "procedure" was remembered in such a way that I was able do it without consciously considering all the steps.

Semantic memory involves remembering concepts, words, facts, data, and other bits of knowledge. When I remember the story of Jesus at the Mount of Transfiguration, I am using semantic memory. If I am asked to recite the Gettysburg address, I am accessing semantic memory. Semantic memory is very important to life and enables me to recall the many pieces of information that have been stored in my brain for use when needed.

Episodic memory is essentially what is involved when we remember an event that occurred in our lives. For example, I remember something that happened at least forty years ago in my grandmother's kitchen. I had gone into her house late one afternoon after basketball practice. I was tired from the workout and upset with the way my coach had treated me. As I entered the kitchen my grandmother was making sugar cookies. The smell was wonderful. I saw the cookies on the table and asked grandma if I could have one. She smiled, said "Sure Bud," and moved to the table to choose one for me. Grandma reached over and took one of those large, sugar-coated cookies from the table and handed it to me. It was warm in my hand. Within seconds after receiving the cookie I took it to my lips, and as I did the aroma was fresh and sweet, full of the scent of vanilla and sugar. I took a bite and it was soft and seemed to melt in my mouth. I remember feeling happy in that moment, and one thing I knew for sure: Grandma's sugar cookies were good and I wanted to eat some more.

Notice all the ingredients of this memory. First, it engaged all five senses. I heard, saw, smelled, touched, and tasted in that one encounter. The episode also elicited feelings of happiness. I engaged in a series of actions, and I derived some meaningful conclusions from it all, including that grandma's sugar cookies were good for me to eat. Unlike procedural memory and semantic memory, episodic memories engage us at many different levels. I can remember that Abraham Lincoln was born in 1809, but the fact does not impact me like the memory of a single sugar cookie. His birth is more important for sure. But an episodic memory is far more subjective, including images, senses, feelings, behaviors, and meaning.

I am convinced that episodic memories are the most powerful type of memories we have because they are filled with senses, feelings, images, actions, and meaning. Traumatic wounds are episodic memories, but in this case overwhelmingly negative. It is very difficult to eliminate the effects of a negative episodic memory through procedural or semantic memory. I am not saying these are unimportant to the process. I am simply saying that they are not powerful enough to free a person from unprocessed emotional upheaval caused by a traumatic episode of the past.

It can be helpful, for example, to learn deep breathing and relaxation techniques as a way of reducing anxiety. And there is great value to gaining insight and knowledge about the problems associated with PTSD, and working to replace old negative messages with new ones. But the only way to actually release the unprocessed emotions of the past and heal traumatic memories is through a more powerful episode. And the powerful new episode that is needed involves

Jesus entering the episodic memory of the past with the broken person. When that happens, the images, senses, feelings, actions, and meanings of the negative past are faced, re-experienced, processed, released, and then overpowered by a new episode with Jesus. That is the essence of the healing of memory through formational prayer. Chapter Six develops that process in detail.

Having said all this, I now come to the important resource of episodic encounters with the Lord, experienced in day-to-day life. People who have been wounded should work to open their senses before the Lord by accessing the power of right brain functions. It will be very difficult to enter negative emotions of the past unless the person is first helped to experience positive episodes with the Lord in the present. The caregiver should encourage those under their care to seek the presence of God in sunsets, and quiet moments, and gentle winds, and children's smiles. They must help them do more than think about God.

Wounded people must be willing, as frightening as it may be, to stay in the present moment, not run from it because they fear being triggered emotionally. It will not be easy, but the Holy Spirit will help. This experience may not come quickly, but God is faithful and wants us to experience his presence more than we desire to encounter him. It all begins by being willing, telling God we are willing, and positioning in the moments of life to "sense" the wonder of his loving presence. The resource of episodic encounters with God in the present—those moments that are filled with senses, feelings, actions, and meaning—become the grand prelude to meeting Jesus in the traumatic episodes of long ago. He waits to meet the broken there, and to forever transform and set them free.

Chapter Six

MEETING CHRIST IN THE WOUNDS OF THE PAST

On the night of the Passover, Jesus went to Gethsemane to be with his disciples and pray. The week had already been highly emotional, and Jesus knew that within hours there would be betrayal, abandonment by his closest friends, trial, public humiliation, scourging, crucifixion, and death. He was in the center of severe traumatic events that would appear, for at least three days, to totally defeat him.

In Gethsemane Jesus poured out his heart to the Father, seeking his presence and direction for the hours ahead. He was experiencing emotional agony and processing indescribable pain and loss. No other passage in all of scripture provides a better understanding of how Jesus responded to traumatic events than this one. This narrative holds the keys to unlocking people from the devastating long term effects of unprocessed pain from a broken past.

The story of Jesus in Gethsemane has provided me with great hope. I am encouraged and humbled knowing that Christ understands what it is like to experience traumatic wounding. He is, as the writer of Hebrews said, able to sympathize with our weaknesses (Hebrews 4:25). Jesus did not come to earth in all his glory, but instead chose to experience life as a human being. He had no special advantages because he was the Son of God. Jesus set all this aside at the incarnation. He felt everything we feel, experienced the pain we experience, and was tempted in all ways. As a result, we can turn to Jesus for help in even the toughest times. When we are trapped in the unprocessed emotional flood of past traumatic wounding, we find in Jesus a compassionate Friend who holds the promise of deep transformation.

Jesus knows what the pain of traumatic wounding is like. He experienced its full force, faced the overwhelming flood, and struggled to stay the course. And now he welcomes us as we turn to him for help and healing. The writer of Hebrews said it best when he wrote: "Let us then approach the throne of grace with confidence, so that we may receive mercy and find grace to help us in our time of need" (Hebrews 4:16). Those who walk this difficult journey need mercy and grace. And Jesus is there, ready and willing to meet every hurting person at the place of deepest need.

Gethsemane

The Gethsemane narrative provides priceless truths about Jesus and traumatic wounding. A careful reading of the story begins to unveil a strategy for care.

They went to a place called Gethsemane, and Jesus said to His disciples, "Sit here while I pray." He took Peter, James, and John along with Him, and he began to be deeply distressed and troubled. "My soul is overwhelmed with sorrow to the point of death," he said to them. "Stay here and keep watch."

Going a little farther, he fell to the ground and prayed that if possible the hour might pass from him. "Abba, Father," he said, "Everything is possible for you. Take this cup from me. Yet not what I will, but what you will."

Then he returned to his disciples and found them sleeping. "Simon," he said to Peter, "are you asleep? Could you not keep watch for one hour? Watch and pray so that you will not fall into temptation. The spirit is willing, but the body is weak."

Once more he went away and prayed the same thing. When he came back, he again found them sleeping, because their eyes were heavy. They did not know what to say to him.

Returning the third time, he said to them, "Are you still sleeping and resting. Enough! The hour has come. Look, the Son of Man is betrayed into the hands of sinners. Rise! Let us go! Here comes my betrayer." (Mark 14:32-42)

Verses 33 and 34 show us the great emotional pain Jesus suffered in Gethsemane. The text says that Jesus was in deep sorrow, even to the point of death. Luke adds to this, saying that Jesus was in anguish and that his sweat was like drops of blood falling to the ground. The emotional trauma was so severe that God sent an angel to strengthen him (Luke 22: 43). The nature of the Lord's experience would not be lost on anyone who battles the effects of traumatic wounding. It captures perfectly what it can be like to be locked in a PTSD episode. But for Jesus, the pain was not coming from an unprocessed event of the past; his anguish was related to a traumatic event very much in the present and still unfolding.

Bearing the weight of all he was facing, Jesus was experiencing a flood of powerful feelings. As Mark recorded, Jesus felt as if he was going to die. He was suffocating in the deep, dark, quickly-rising emotional waters of grief and fear. He repeatedly asked God to save him from the cup of suffering, to please make another way. The struggle in Gethsemane was, to say the least, a living hell.

People who battle the effects of traumatic wounding know these feelings well. It is the emotional drowning I described earlier. Those who are locked in an emotional episode can feel as if they are dying. And they begin to panic. The anguish and grief is so intense that they fear they might never make it through. Like Jesus, they cry out in desperation for some kind of help. I know I have. On more than one occasion I begged and pleaded for God to stop the pain. I honestly believed I could not take one more moment of the battle. One more little splash and I would be done. That's the way a traumatic episode is—dark and debilitating.

The deep anguish Jesus experienced was not the only sign of his traumatic struggle. Luke wrote that sweat dripped from Jesus like blood falling to the ground. A traumatic episode does more than affect the emotions. The body begins to respond and often people feel physically out of control. In a PTSD episode, they can sweat profusely, tremble, experience chest pains, shortness of breath, tightening muscles, and dizziness. I have, more often than I want to admit, experienced the terror of cold sweats and body tremors. I have fought to breathe, felt my body grow tense, and feared I might faint. And all I could do was wonder how long it was going to last and how bad was it going to get.

When bodily responses begin to occur, panic and fear only increase. People's emotions and body begin working in tandem against them. A traumatic encounter does feel like an anguish leading to death. Thankfully, Jesus knows very well what the struggle is all about. He faced it that night on the Mount of Olives. And he is more than willing to face it again with wounded people. That is the promise and hope of freedom that comes from the Gethsemane account.

Moving into the Pain

It is important to note that Jesus processed the traumatic experience as it occurred. He did not wait until it all passed, then try to deal with it when he was more in control. He stayed in the storm until the emotions were processed and he received strength and release from God. This point is very important to helping the broken and must not be minimized. The best time to work on overwhelming emotions of the past is when people are triggered and the flood is actually occurring. It is certainly not the only time to work with people on the effects of traumatic wounding. But it does provide an excellent opportunity for uncovering the unprocessed wounds of the past.

Admittedly, I do not like to work on past memories when I have been triggered. The feelings seem too powerful and I want to distance, disconnect, and come back to them when I am more in control. In Chapter Two I shared my experience of being triggered when my son left our home in South Carolina to return to Ohio. And, if you remember, I mentioned that I was locked in a PTSD episode for three days before I received help. The truth is I could have called out for help the first day. But I didn't. I was ashamed and embarrassed to be there again. I did not want to walk any deeper into the emotional flood. The waves were too high and the undertow too strong. I was intending to withdraw and just wait it out, even though I knew better. It was my wife who contacted someone for help, not me.

I understand why people want to wait until later to deal with unprocessed pain. Like me, they are embarrassed, ashamed, and often afraid. Withdrawing and waiting seems to be the best and most natural choice. But that is a mistake. The time to deal with it is when triggered.

The moment feels almost evil. It is dark, confusing, and filled with overpowering negative emotions. But it can turn and become a gift from the Lord. It is the perfect time to ask Jesus to walk into the memory and help a person experience release. Long ago the wounded person had distanced from his or her feelings. And ever since, the unprocessed and unreleased feelings have remained jammed up inside. In a PTSD experience, the past becomes suddenly present. It is then that the person has an opportunity to process and release emotions bottled up inside them.

Unfortunately most people are not aware of what is happening, so they fail to go into the moment as an opportunity for healing. But if they or their caregiver are willing, the traumatic episode can be encountered and then replaced with a new episode with Christ. The Lord, by walking through his personal traumatic experience in Gethsemane, is able to walk with others through traumatic woundings of the past. There can be deep transformation and healing when the past is faced with Jesus.

Positioning the Broken through Formational Prayer

For almost fifteen years I have been humbled to have the opportunity to position many wonderful people before the Lord for the healing of memories. I never would have dreamed that Jesus could use my own journey as he has. But through the outpouring of his matchless grace and mercy, the wounds I experienced have enabled me to turn and help others. The words of Paul in 2 Corinthians have become a reality:

> Praise be to the God and Father of our Lord Jesus Christ, the Father of compassion and the God of all comfort, who comforts us in all our troubles, so that we can comfort those in any trouble with the comfort we ourselves have received from God. For just as the sufferings of Christ flow into our lives, so also through Christ our comfort overflows. (Corinthians 1:3-5)

God cares about those who are struggling with the effects of past traumatic events. As this passage states, matchless comfort comes to all who turn to Christ Jesus in faith. His sufferings have opened the way for healing. And in the case of traumatic events, his battle in Gethsemane has made a way for our victory. Jesus made provision for healing in the Garden of Gethsemane, and he himself has provided a path to obtain that healing. I have followed that path myself and often met Jesus there. I have been able to see many other caregivers help the broken find release and freedom by following His example.

The guidelines I will share are just that—guidelines. They are not part of a magical formula, nor should they be followed with a strict, inflexible attitude. Instead, under the gentle guidance of the Holy Spirit, wounded people and their caregivers can find in these steps a process for meeting Jesus. I intend to discuss each step and illustrate it when appropriate. But before doing so, several reminders are in order.

First, caregivers should remember that their personal spiritual life matters in this process. Love for Christ and openness to the Spirit is foundational to all of life, no less so when helping a wounded person find healing. Prayer and spiritual preparation are essential to ministering to people using the formational prayer model. This is not a ministry for the uncommitted and unskilled. The caregiver role demands adequate preparation and commitment.

Second, the resources discussed in Chapter Four and Chapter Five are important to the process. Time must be taken to address each so that a hurting people can draw from them on the journey to healing.

Third, seldom, if ever, will the process defined here happen in a single session of formational prayer. Formational prayer is a process and it happens best in the context of an ongoing relationship with an anointed caregiver. It is a critical part of a much larger relationship of care that includes dialogue, instruction, direction, and appropriate assignments. And even with the actual practice of formational prayer, it is not unusual for it to involve a series of sessions.

Freedom and release often come one step at a time as the Holy Spirit addresses the wounds, false beliefs, emotional upheaval, and dysfunctional behaviors that are tightly woven together. I try to remind people that Jesus is in charge of the process and we follow his lead. Movement toward freedom is the goal, regardless of the pace. With sanctification, the process of becoming like Jesus, the journey is as important as the destination. And when walking with Jesus into the memories of the past, each step along the path is an opportunity for people to experience deep transformation. For me, the greatest gift of all has been developing a deeper relationship with him. Healing is wonderful, but intimacy with the Lord is the matchless treasure of life.

What follows is an eight-step strategy that can, when empowered by the Holy Spirit, position people to meet Jesus in a past traumatic event. Rooted in the experience of Jesus in Gethsemane, it is a biblically sound way for wounded people to experience the healing of memories. I am choosing to address what follows to caregivers. However, people who are seeking healing and interested in this process should understand these steps and look for caregivers who are gifted and skilled in the formational prayer model. The eight steps are:

- Step One: Establish an atmosphere conducive to the process of formational prayer.

- Step Two: Provide the necessary support.

- Step Three: Prioritize safety.

- Step Four: Position the person before the Lord.

- Step Five: Encourage the open expression of feelings about struggling with PTSD and other related disorders.

- Step Six: Ask the Holy Spirit to identify the original source of the emotional upheaval.

- Step Seven: Help the person tell the story of the traumatic event.

- Step Eight: Position the person for a new episodic encounter with Jesus.

Step One: Establish an Atmosphere Conducive to the Process of Formational Prayer

Jesus did not process his pain in the highly charged atmosphere of Jerusalem. Instead, he took his disciples and went to the Garden of Gethsemane. He got away from the people and pressures of the city to find space and solitude far more conducive to meeting God. The Garden of Gethsemane was a familiar spot where Jesus retreated with his closest followers.

The environment was peaceful, surrounded by the sights, smells, and sounds of God's creation. It appealed to "right brain" sensitivities, a critical resource when seeking to connect relationally, spiritually, and emotionally with the Father. Jesus did not just happen to go to Gethsemane, he chose to go there. And I believe he went there for good reason. It was the perfect place to deal with the flood of feelings that were threatening to undo him.

There is no better place for me to meet the Lord in the memories of the past than at my friend's farm. In my opinion, it is the most lovely setting in the entire area, almost picture perfect. I love to experience formational prayer out in the barn by the large sliding door, looking out across a large open field. Over the years the field has been full of pumpkins or corn, or sometimes wheat. Regardless of the time of year, it is a feast for the senses. I have been praying and seen a deer pass by, watched an oriole move in and out of her nest, and sat in silence as a small rabbit fed on the clover near the corner of the barn. It is my Gethsemane. It is a place where I have often retreated from the pressures of life to meet the Lord in prayer. Being there did not take me out of the flood of emotions. It simply provided a setting conducive to meeting Jesus through formational prayer.

Hurting people should experience formational prayer in an environment that opens the senses for an encounter with God. It is critical that caregivers provide a place where people can move away from the pressures of normal day-to-day life. Caregivers should pay attention to aesthetics, decorating in a way that appeals to the senses. Pictures, soft music, scented candles, comfortable chairs, and proper lighting can help provide an environment conducive to a Gethsemane type encounter. If caregivers can possibly meet with people in a retreat setting, all the better. A clinical atmosphere of desks, filing cabinets, telephones, and fluorescent lights often causes unnecessary anxiety and should be avoided at all costs.

Step Two: Provide the Necessary Support.

One of the saddest parts of the Gethsemane story involves the Lord's three best friends, Peter, James, and John (Mark 14:33 and 34). All the disciples except Judas went with Jesus to Gethsemane. But once there, Jesus went off to process his emotional pain and asked Peter, James, and John to go with him. They saw that Jesus was in deep anguish and fear, and the Lord wanted their support during this dark and agonizing time. But they were not there for Jesus; they fell asleep, leaving Jesus to struggle alone before God.

My heart breaks when I meet wounded people who do not have any support. The journey through PTSD, as well as other distortions and disorders, is already horribly difficult. But when traveled alone, people can find it almost impossible to press on. I well remember entering the psychiatric hospital and having only one friend visit, even though many former colleagues lived in the city where the hospital was located. I knew they were aware of what happened to me and that I was there for treatment. But not a visit or a word arrived from any of them. Their support could have made a difference, but it was not there. And my experience is multiplied many times over for countless people who do not have support. Friends, families, church member, pastors, and caregivers must become far more sensitive to the needs of the emotionally broken, and develop networks of support so that none need make this difficult journey alone.

I also know what it is like to have support in a time of deep emotional distress. It has enabled me to find strength and confidence enough to move into even the darkest places of the past. More than once people have held me fast when I thought I would surely go down into the depths of dark waters and never again come up. Deeply anointed people positioned me to meet Jesus in the places of past pain, stayed at my side as the emotions were released and processed, and walked with me to the other side. Their support was priceless, and I owe a debt to them that I can never repay.

People seeking healing need to be supported by family, friends, churches, pastors, and most certainly their caregivers. Such support is a priceless gift that brings much-needed safety into the healing moment.

Step Three: Prioritize Safety

A significant amount of time was taken in Chapter Three to discuss the resource of safety. I want to re-emphasize that need and share a few thoughts as they relate to the process of formational prayer. The people seeking help must come to trust their caregivers. It is that simple. Trust is the foundation upon which the entire process builds. And in most cases trust is earned, not given. It may take some time, but broken people must become confident that their caregivers will not intentionally harm them in any way. That does not mean caregivers must be perfect. They may make mistakes. But wounded people need to see that their caregivers can keep a confidence, protect them from unnecessary embarrassment, and move through the process with grace and mercy.

There is an additional consideration. In Chapter Four I discussed the safe place exercise. This exercise is foundational to the formational prayer process and caregivers should take time to instruct those they serve in its importance and in how to engage in the exercise. For some people it will not come easily. But that will not be true for everyone. Hopefully the caregiver will have already assigned this exercise to the person before the formational prayer sessions begin and will have monitored their progress. The actual formational prayer sessions should begin with the safe place exercise. I want a broken person to allow the Spirit to use that internal safe place as the place where he re-experiences the emotions of past woundings. This provides a resource of strength for the process. Emotions will run high during the session. By entering the memory from the safe place within, the person is able to remain secure even while touching the pain of the past.

When I am receiving help, I ask the Spirit to take me to the safe place where he has been meeting me for some time. There I spend time experiencing the Lord's presence and delight. Then I allow the Spirit to lead me into a memory and open myself to re-experiencing the unprocessed pain of the past. If the emotions begin to run high, I can re-access my safe place, tell the Lord about my feelings, and receive the provision I need to re-enter the memory with him. Doing this has reduced an amazing amount of anxiety. I have come to the place where I know he is there, in my safe place, waiting to help throughout the session.

Step Four: Position the Person before the Lord

When the time came for Jesus to process the pain that was flooding his emotions, he turned to God in prayer. Jesus lifted his concern to his Heavenly Father, seeking the help that only he could provide. I am not saying that he did not talk with anyone else about what was bothering Him. There is no evidence that tells whether he did or did not. But what I do know is that the Jesus dealt with his pain before God, and we should learn from that example.

Transformation demands a supernatural encounter with God. I have great appreciation for the skills and techniques of effective counselors. They have an ability to help people connect with the details of their own story, access their own internal resources to gain strength, and discover a pathway out of problems that they were not aware they even knew. Gifted counselors can provide invaluable insight on the nature of a problem, as well as help people develop plans for ongoing well-being. All of this is vital to the counseling process.

But release from the wounds of past traumatic events takes more than dialogue between a counselor and client. It demands the power of God. So the caregiver gently helps position the broken person before the Lord. If Jesus needed to meet the Father in prayer as part of processing pain, certainly we do as well.

I once had a Christian counselor who, when I asked him to pray, said he did not do that with clients. I found a different counselor. I am well aware that some caregivers do not bring the Lord directly into sessions. Some are uncomfortable with prayer, and others feel constrained by their agency's policies and state laws. I certainly believe a caregiver must never impose prayer or God on anyone. But I am also convinced that God alone, though Christ, holds the key to healing and release from wounds of the past. Broken people need a context to do as Jesus did. They should be helped with the prayer, "Abba, Father, everything is possible for you!"

Positioning people before the Lord is not a complicated process. I simply invite a person into his or her safe place and give time for the person to rest in the presence of the Lord. When led of the Holy Spirit, I invite the person to ask the Lord to be with them through the remainder of the session. I tell them that everything we do will be done in God's presence, and that it is important that the person share what they are feeling, sensing, and "seeing" in their creative imagination, telling both me and the Lord about it all. My role is to watch, be open to the Spirit's leading, encourage the person to stay present with the Lord throughout the session, and do what I can to keep the process on track.

Step Five: Encourage the Open Expression of Feelings about PTSD and Other Related Disorders

At Calvary Jesus made a way so that all lost people could be reconciled with the Father. That redemption was the very reason Jesus came to earth. Through Christ's death God made it possible for every person to be transformed and set free from the bondage of darkness and evil. Jesus willingly gave his life on the cross so that people can receive the blessings of that sacrifice.

Yet people dare not forget that the agony of Gethsemane was so intense that Jesus thought he might die of anguish. Jesus poured out his feelings before the Father and told him exactly what was bothering him. Jesus asked if there was any way that he could be released from the cup of suffering. Jesus openly shared his concern with God, and then waited for the help only the Father could provide. Caregivers should encourage wounded people to share their feelings openly and honestly. What follows are several suggestions that may help people express their feelings and tell their stories to God.

After having helped a person meet God in the Spirit-directed safe place, the caregiver should invite the broken person to tell God about what he or she is feeling. Having been triggered by some event, and struggling with overwhelming emotions, the person talks to God honestly. For me, that meant holding nothing back. I remember well letting God know that I was afraid, tired, and living in constant agony. I told him that I was sick of living in anxiety and the unrelenting flood of emotions that come with PTSD. I expressed anger and I

unflinchingly asked why God allowed me to languish in such a horrible place of pain and darkness. I was as honest and emotional as a
psalmist, expressing every frustrating and debilitating thing about
being triggered yet again and locked in a place of unspeakable emotional overload.

Such openness and honesty is not only appropriate, it is necessary. Instead of trying to suppress all that is going on within, broken
people should be encouraged to express their feelings with all the
energy that is welled up inside.

Many people were raised or still live in dysfunctional homes where
feelings were not processed well. Some people would have been
restricted from sharing openly about their hurts and heartaches.
Others were brought up in families where feelings were expressed
in very damaging ways. Caregivers should give basic instructions
about how to express emotions, particularly during formational
prayer sessions.

I give people permission to express their feelings during any session. I assure them that it is right, and good, and acceptable. I want
them not only to say what they are feeling, but actually to express
those feelings. If they need to cry or shout or lie on the floor or pace
back and forth, fine. But I ask them not to break anything in my office
or hurt me in any way. And I remind them that formational prayer
sessions take place in the presence of God, so emotions should flow
up to him.

Not all people are able to get in touch with their feelings. Often I
will ask them to write a lament to God. I invite them to be absolutely
honest and never censor their feelings. God is able to receive people's
emotions, even when directed at him. Sometimes I give the lament as
an assignment between sessions. At other times, I ask people to write
during our time together. I then invite them to read their lament to
the Lord.

Step Six: Identify the Original Source of the Emotional Upheaval

Supported by my caregiver, I was speaking honestly to God about my feelings and frustrations about yet again being locked in a PTSD episode. At the appropriate point my caregiver invited me to ask God to show me where the emotional overload, triggered by an insignificant event, actually originated. My caregiver could see that unprocessed pain from the past was pouring into today and that I needed God's help in identifying its source. Honestly, when she first said that, I got angry. I didn't want to face the past. But eventually I did as suggested. Returning to my safe place which had been created within by the Spirit, I asked the Lord to help me see the source of the present pain. The caregiver supported me in prayer as I waited before the Lord. Slowly my mind was drawn to an event that had occurred almost a decade past. It happened in California while I was pastoring a large congregation. All the specific details are not important to retell, except to say that it involved betrayal and accusation. It was immediately clear that the Lord had identified an unprocessed traumatic wound of the past. And before I could move forward to experience him anew, I needed to meet him in my unprocessed past.

The Lord helps a wounded person find the source of unprocessed emotions. He is willing to lead the broken to the specific places of traumatic wounding. It may take time and great discernment, but eventually the Spirit will unlock the past. Some people may not remember actual events, but simply have feelings that originate from some unconscious memory. Those feelings must be validated and brought to the Lord, even though the person may never actually remember what caused them.

A woman once told me that she had lived her entire life feeling that she was never heard. It was not that her family or friends paid no attention to her. She simply lived with a chronic feeling of being ignored. Through prayer she was able to take those feelings to the

Lord and experience his unconditional love and undivided attention. That episodic encounter brought healing to her and the chronic feelings lifted, even without a memory being attached to the emotions. When a person was wounded as an infant or small child, the specific memory may not surface. But for most people, the memory of traumatic events will surface with the Lord's help.

Step Seven: Help the Person Tell the Story of the Traumatic Event

Even as a boy I was intrigued by the story of Jesus sweating drops of blood. I had heard it in Sunday school and it stuck in mind for the longest time. I could hardly imagine the pain that Jesus must have experienced that would cause him to sweat drops of blood. Many years later, after having become a Christian, I was even more touched by the story. But instead of fascination, I was deeply moved by the love of Christ, that he would face such pain for me. Whether Jesus actually sweated blood or his sweat dropped to the ground like blood does not matter. What does matter is that it was a time of incredible anguish. And rather than hold back the tears, putting on a good front for his followers, Jesus let the emotion pour out before the Father. Even though Christ was God's Messiah, he was honest about his feelings and cried out to God in desperation. Jesus invites broken people to do the same, and willingly enters their pain to bring release and healing.

Wounded people need to get in touch with the pain of the traumatic event that God has identified during a formational prayer session. Reentering a memory in order to process the wounds of the past does not mean the people simply think about what happened. It means they allow the feelings of the event, not processed long ago, to be felt again. It is a matter of allowing oneself to open the senses and connect with the feelings related to the event.

The psychologist Endel Tulving developed the theory of episodic memory discussed in the previous chapter. He believed that it was a unique state of consciousness that allows the "rememberer" to be a "mental time traveler" able to relive a past event. According to Tulving, it does not matter if the event happened last night, last week, or fifty years ago, the person can re-experience what happened as though he or she was free from the constraints of space and time.[10] People will experience the feelings they would have had at the chronological and psychological age they occurred. If wounded in childhood, people do not look back at the event and then feel what they would as adults. The feelings will be far more primitive and small. That may be uncomfortable, but it is a very important part of the process of healing.

A traumatic wound of the past is an episodic memory. It has all the ingredients of sight, sensation, feelings, action, and meaning. Episodic memory is very powerful, affecting what people believe about themselves, others, and God. At this point in the process, caregivers should invite people to tell the Lord about past events identified by the Lord. Again, the exchange is between people and God, with caregivers there in support.

As the person tells God about the experience, the caregiver might help by inviting the individual to:

- Share the picture that comes to mind when recalling the event.

- Express any feelings that were present then and now as the person re-enter the memory.

- Tell God about what he or she was "sensing" as it occurred.

- Talk about the actions that took place that caused the wound.

- Reveal any false beliefs and meanings that resulted from the event.

The person should be encouraged to keep his or her feelings and senses open. In the retelling of the story, the person is able to re-experience the sensations and feelings of the past event. The caregiver should encourage the person to stay with the feelings. In most cases the feelings locked inside begin to pour out before God. Like Jesus, the individual experiences the anguish of the soul, but in this case it comes from an unprocessed event of the past.

The caregiver should seek to maintain a very delicate balance. The person should be free to express all the deep feelings of pain. The un-grieved losses should be allowed to flow if the person is to find freedom. There will often be significant discomfort and emotional pain, which is an important part of the process. At the same time, the caregiver needs to keep the person safe and with the Lord. The broken person needs to feel Jesus' presence, his support, and his grace through the process. The caregiver should regularly check in as the person moves forward, making sure that the individual is connected to the Lord and able to access their safe place. In many cases, this re-telling and re-experiencing happens over time. A single session may not be enough. The caregiver should follow the Spirit's leading, moving forward and stopping at his direction.

When the Lord revealed the wound that happened in California, it connected with me immediately. When the event had originally occurred I worked to keep a good face on it all. I was in my "stoic" phase and wanted people to see my strengths, not my weaknesses. Back then, I saw feelings as weakness. The situation, which went on for several months, was deeply wounding. I was betrayed by a friend and it had legal ramifications. In addition, another particularly close friend had an opportunity to support me, yet did nothing. While in the end everything turned out in my favor, the long season of stress and heartache took a tremendous toll.

For almost ten years I had put it all away—or so I thought. But on this occasion, when triggered so suddenly and experiencing so much emotional overload, the past was very much present. With my caregiver's help I was able to tell the story to the Lord. I shared every honest feeling of anger and resentment that I had back then. The tears flowed. Throughout the time of formational prayer I felt the Lord's presence, and I knew he was right there with me in the moment. He entered my episodic memory, enabling me to process a great deal of pent up pain.

A word of caution. There is definitely a right way and wrong way to approach re-experiencing traumatic events. Imagine for a moment that there is an overfilled balloon and someone intends to let the air out with plans to re-use the balloon at another time. The process should be done so as to get the air out by controlled deflation, not sudden explosion. Controlled deflation will insure that the balloon can be used again, where explosion renders that balloon completely unusable. So it is with processing pent-up emotions caused by traumatic events. It is possible to position broken people before the Lord so that they may experience a controlled release of the past feelings. But it is also possible, given the highly emotional nature of most traumatic memories, that people could re-experience the event to such a degree that they will become afraid and disoriented. That happens when the caregiver has not provided adequate safeguards for the experience. It is both irresponsible and potentially traumatizing in itself.

As people process feelings with the Lord, caregivers should insure that necessary safeguards are in place. These include:

• Encouraging the person to bring someone with them who can provide support during the sessions.

• Assuring the person that you will only go as far as he or she is comfortable and that you will stop at anytime.

- Making sure the person is in a safe place with the Lord as the very first step in the process—and able to return there whenever the emotions seem too intense to handle.

- Regularly asking questions like, "How are you doing? Can you sense the Lord with you in this? Do you need to stop for a while, or can you keep going?"

- Staying focused and dependent upon the Holy Spirit's presence through the process.

- Maintaining eye contact, communicating calm, compassion, and confidence.

- Using appropriate touch to show support.

- Providing symbolic objects to hold, if he or she desires, that remind of God's presence in the process (a cross, crucifix, blanket, etc.).

- Constantly reminding the person of the Lord's presence and, when appropriate, speaking specific scriptures on the promised presence and protection of God.

These simple safeguards can go a long way toward insuring that the process of re-experiencing will be a healing experience for broken people.

Step Eight: Position the Person for a New Episodic Encounter with Jesus

There came a moment in Gethsemane when the Lord obviously experienced the presence of the Father, experienced his love, received his direction, and found peace. He arose from prayer, ready for the events of the passion to unfold. He was not simply resigned to his fate. Jesus had received the provision of the Father's grace and was able to move ahead in confidence and strength. It was settled for Jesus. The cross was the Father's will and Jesus said yes. He said yes to God and yes for us. At some point in the agony of Gethsemane, Jesus had an episodic encounter with the Father. The anguish was now gone, and the Word spoken into Christ's heart brought him to his feet, ready to face the path ahead.

I believe that the Lord desires to bring a new episodic memory to the broken. He desires to encounter the person in a new episode of truth, transformation, and life. I have experienced this many times along the path of healing. It is the encounter that turns darkness to light, replaces evil with good, and exchanges grief for joy. As I engaged the Lord in the wounding of accusation, betrayal and abandonment, an amazing thing happened: during the formational prayer I experienced Jesus in a way I had never even considered.

As I was describing the event to the Lord and the caregiver, I suddenly "saw" myself sitting in the church office all alone. I was suffocating from all the stress of the situation, and was wondering if I it would ever end. The office was dimly lit and it was dark outside. I am sure that was symbolic of how I was feeling at the time. I was angry. And I was depressed because no one seemed to care about how I was doing. At my caregiver's invitation, I asked Jesus to enter the memory with me. In my mind's eye I saw Jesus, not in the office, but hanging on the cross. His head was limp, as though he were already dead. But as I looked at him on the cross, he slowly lifted his head and spoke these words, "I care." Right there and then, I began to cry from a place deep within. But, unlike before, these were tears of release, astonishment, and indescribable joy.

With those words, the sadness and anger passed. It did not matter so much how others had treated me. Jesus cared! And as that grace flooded my soul, I was able to extend release and forgiveness. I had an episodic experience that was far more powerful than the past trauma. I encountered the living Christ and he cared about what happened to me. And he cared for me. I had known that in my head for years. But this was the Lord, in the memory with me, speaking the truth into my heart. It was an overwhelming spiritual experience. I was present with Jesus and he was present with me. I had a new, more powerful episodic encounter, and it was with Jesus.

Caregivers should, at the initiation of the Holy Spirit, ask the person they are helping to invite Christ into the memory being processed. Allowing the Holy Spirit to use his or her creative imagination, the Spirit will create a picture of Jesus moving into the wound of the past. There he will communicate, through word or deed, the truth of his love, care, and involvement. While the caregiver should not be quick to interject his own thoughts, he must be watchful for any distractions or distortions that come from the evil one. As the wounded person opens up to the presence of Christ, a new episodic encounter is formed within the heart. The truth of Christ's loving involvement in the person's life, past present, and future, will transform and set the person free.

Earlier in this book I confessed that I am on an ongoing journey toward transformation and freedom. I have experienced much healing, yet there is still much for me to experience. But the wonderful faithfulness of Christ bids me onward in the process. Building upon what he has done, I remain positioned for what he yet wants to do. So it will be for others. The Lord will meet the broken in the dark and debilitating wounds of the past. He will lovingly receive the feelings of the unprocessed past, and hold them dear to his heart. And he will speak of his everlasting love and constant care.

Chapter Seven

THE HELPER

Jesus had spent the day teaching at the water's edge. A large crowd had gathered, so Jesus stood in a boat and taught the people many things about God. He told a story about a farmer sowing seeds on different types of soil, illustrating how the same seed, falling on different soils, produces a radically different harvest. Later, he gathered with his disciples and explained the story, then told them other secrets of the Kingdom of God. He said that God's kingdom was like a seed planted deep in the ground, and that over time it grows from stalk, to head, to full kernel. And he told a parable about a tiny mustard seed that, when planted, becomes the largest plant in the garden. Mark said that Jesus did not teach them anything that day except through parables (Mark 4:1-33).

As evening came Jesus invited the disciples to leave the crowds behind and cross the lake to the other side. They got into a boat and began to sail across, when suddenly they were caught in a furious storm that seemed to arise out of nowhere. The waves were so severe that they crashed over the boat, filling it with so much water that it nearly capsized. The disciples were terrified, fighting for their lives.

As this drama was unfolding, Jesus was sound asleep in the bow resting upon a cushion. The disciples were in a panic and jostled Jesus awake yelling, "Teacher, don't you care if we drown?" Jesus simply stands up, commands the wind and waves, "Be Quiet! Be Still!" and everything returned to complete calm. Jesus asked the disciples why they were so afraid. Frankly, I can totally understand why they were afraid. They thought they were going to drown in the strong winds and crashing waves. It seems like a very natural reaction to me. But Jesus links their fear to a basic lack of faith. Interestingly, the disciples were even more terrified after Jesus calmed the storm than they were when the seas were raging. They were shocked by the authority and power of Christ. They looked at each other and asked, "Who is this? Even the winds and waves obey him!" (Mark 4:35 -41).

This story has become a source of incredible hope to me. While an actual historical event, it serves as a metaphor of Christ's faithfulness when caught in the overwhelming challenges of the journey I am taking. There will be high winds and waves. And many times I will feel as if I am about to capsize and drown. I will probably find myself at times asking Jesus, "Don't you care if I drown?" I will say those words all the while knowing that Jesus has shown his love and care for me innumerable times. It will be the fear speaking. But when I do it will be words spoken out of desperation. And at times like that, I will be reminded of this story in Mark 4. And I will hear Jesus whisper, "Have a little faith."

I am immensely grateful that the Lord does not require fully matured faith before he will act. When the disciples were unable to heal a boy possessed of demons, Jesus challenged their faith. He then said that it only takes faith the size of a mustard seed to tell a mountain to move and it will move. Jesus then said that "nothing will be impossible for you" (Matthew 17:20 and 21)! It only takes a little faith, humbly offered to the Lord, to see great things happen.

Jesus was not rebuking his disciples in the story of the stilling of the sea because they did not have faith to believe that he could rebuke a great storm. Nor am I convinced that Jesus was trying to get them to exercise their own faith and speak to the storm themselves. Jesus wanted them to be confident of this one fact: he would get them to the promised destination. He had invited them to go to the other side with him, and no storm, no matter how great, was going to keep them from getting there. And that is the hope that holds me fast on my own journey of healing. Jesus has promised to be with me always and he will see me through to the other side of this disorder, where freedom and transformation await.

This Is a Journey

Freedom and release from wounds of the past do not happen through a one time event. I honestly wish they did. It is a process that happens over time. It involves many different channels of healing, including spiritual exercises, support, counseling, formational prayer, and other activities that position the broken for the touch of Jesus. As I said earlier, I am both healed and being healed. That is the nature of this process. I am also convinced that it happens over time because the journey itself transforms us into the likeness of Christ. And with God, that is more important than anything else life has to offer. We are, by the Spirit, continually being changed to be like Jesus. This healing process contributes to that transformation, developing the virtues and values of the Lord deep within our hearts.

Few, if any, people are struggling in life simply because of one unprocessed event of the past. Granted, there may be one major traumatic wound at the heart of all the turmoil and upheaval. But from my experience, both personal and professional, the greater wound or wounds are normally connected to lesser ones that also need attention. I not only suffered from some pretty dramatic childhood trauma, I experienced a number of other significant, less stressful events that have also taken a toll on my well being. Added to that, all these events, be they greatly traumatic or less so, have been inter-twined with false beliefs, un-grieved losses, and various dysfunctional behaviors that are complex and distorting in my life.

Even after a healing encounter with Christ in a past memory, other issues need attention, involving spiritual direction, counsel, and additional prayer. Healing life's hurts is a journey that often involves strong winds and crashing waves, and it takes time and commitment to get to the other side. There are wonderful moments along the way when, through an encounter with Christ, calm and peace comes to us at the command of Jesus. Those are sweet releases along the journey of transformation. But it must be clear that we are talking about a healing journey, not a healing event.

Jesus has promised never to leave or forsake us along the path (Hebrews 13:5). We will, like the disciples, make it to the other side, regardless of the strength of the winds and the ferocity of the waves. Jesus has sent a Helper, who will bring us incredible strength and comfort as we learn to depend upon him. This Helper has been called by many names: Comforter, Counselor, even the Flame of Love. He is the Holy Spirit, and he has been promised to fill all of God's children. All we need to do is open our hearts and ask.

The Holy Spirit

If someone were to ask me the single most important resource needed for the journey to freedom, I would say without hesitation, the ministry of the Holy Spirit. He has helped me all along the way, and has worked changes in my life I never dreamed possible. He has brought an intimate and experiential dimension to my relationship with Christ. The Spirit, who indwelled my heart at conversion, has been faithful to renew and cleanse me at so many levels that it defies understanding. And even now the Spirit is at work in me to continue that process, preparing the way for Jesus to bring transformation in the yet un-surrendered places deep inside my soul. Words cannot adequately describe my dependence upon the Holy Spirit's constant care. He is, by grace, God alive in me. One of my deepest prayers is simply, "Please give me a greater capacity for your presence in my life, dear Flame of Love."

All Christians can benefit from a deeper understanding and openness to the Holy Spirit. But here, I want to emphasize the Spirit's relation to those broken by wounds of the past, and to the men and women who help them. Neither group dare make the journey without the infilling presence of the Spirit. It is not only unwise to do so, it is impossible. The way is too dark, the waters too deep, the waves too high, and the winds too strong to be successfully navigated alone. Both wounded people and caregivers alike need help. And simply stated, that is why Jesus sent the Holy Spirit. He is our Divine Helper.

Caregivers need the Spirit's help, not only personally but professionally. Regardless of the level of training and ability, caregivers will need the direction, insight, and discernment that only the Spirit can bring. Helping broken people recover from the effects of traumatic wounding is a serious responsibility. The caregiver will be helping people move through places of darkness where the evil one seeks to do great harm. Many will be struggling with false beliefs and wrestling with serious dysfunctional behaviors. Finding freedom and release requires that people be able to encounter Christ in the memories of the past. Any one of these facts should motivate caregivers to seek more of the Spirit's anointing for this ministry.

Those wounded by traumatic events of the past need the Spirit's help as well. It is difficult living with the effects of traumatic events that have remained unprocessed. Emotions run high and life can get very hard to figure out. The temptation to kill all the pain is at times unbearable. More than a few wounded people have become addicted to all kinds of "painkillers." Shame and embarrassment are, for many, constant companions. It makes no sense to put a pretty face on this struggle. It can be a hellish nightmare. All to say, those living with the distortions and disorders resulting from traumatic events need serious help. And Jesus has provided that help in the person of the Holy Spirit.

There have been times when I have stood outside a classroom and felt almost uncontrollable anxiety, and yet knew I had to enter and teach. In my strength I knew that it would be very difficult to get through the three hours, let alone say something worth remembering. But a simple prayer, asking the Holy Spirit to be my Helper, invariably enabled me to go to my post and serve the Lord. Many times I have felt an empowerment and presence assuring me that I was not in the moment alone. The anxiety did not necessarily leave, nor was I sailing in still waters. But the Spirit heard my cry, and saw me through to the end. He longs to help and even a whispered prayer will unleash His care.

Jesus and the Holy Spirit

Consider the degree to which Jesus depended on the Holy Spirit. Every aspect of his life and ministry were intricately interconnected with the Spirit. The incarnation of Christ began when the Holy Spirit hovered over Mary at conception (Luke 1:35). After his birth, Jesus was presented at the temple where Simeon, filled with the Holy Spirit, gave praise to God for allowing him to see the Messiah (Luke 2:25-32). The Holy Spirit, in the form of a dove, descended upon Jesus at his baptism and God declared him the beloved Son (Luke 3:22). Jesus then went out into the desert at the leading of the Holy Spirit, where he was tempted by the evil one for forty days (Luke 4:1).

At the beginning of his ministry, Jesus went into the synagogue and was handed a scroll in order to read a passage of scripture (Luke 4:18 and 19). He selected the text from Isaiah 61 that begins, "The Spirit of the Lord is upon me because he has anointed me to preach good news to the poor" (Isaiah 61:1). Jesus was God's anointed servant and went from there to preach, heal, and deliver people from demons, all in the power of the Holy Spirit. Every miracle, healing, teaching, sermon, and deliverance was accomplished in harmony with the Spirit's presence. If Jesus, the Son of God, was so intricately connected to the Spirit, would it not then be even more important that we be filled with the Spirit's presence and power?

Some people might think that the ministry of the Spirit is reserved for spiritual superstars. That could not be further from the truth. Jesus has given the Helper to all his followers, from the first moments of their relationship with him. And, they can seek a deeper awareness and experience of the Holy Spirit if they only ask. Jesus once said, "If you then, though you are evil, know how to give good gifts to your children, how much more will your Father in heaven give the Holy Spirit to those who ask" (Luke 11:13). This text should move caregivers, and those who struggle with the effects of deep wounding, to turn immediately to God in prayer, seeking the good gift their heavenly Father longs to give.

Our Strength Is Not Enough

I want to return briefly to Gethsemane and several of the events that occurred that night. In a single twenty-four hour period the forces of darkness broke loose upon Jesus with a vengeance. It was a time of great violence against the Lord, and not a shining moment for his followers. Twelve men who had spent three years with Jesus essentially deserted him when things got tough. Even though they had heard his teachings, witnessed his miracles, and experienced his power, they were not a force of strength and faithfulness when the passion began to unfold. Judas betrayed Jesus, selling him out for thirty pieces of silver (Matthew 26:14-16). Peter, James, and John failed to support the Lord during his anguish in Gethsemane (Mark 14:32-42).

When a crowd sent from the religious leaders came to arrest Jesus, one of them drew a sword and cut off a man's ear, much to the dismay of the Lord (Luke 22:47-53). Mark wrote that at that moment, "everyone deserted him and fled," with one man running into the night completely naked (Mark 14:50-52). Peter did follow Jesus at a distance, and as the Lord was being tried, sat with some guards to warm his hands by a fire. A servant girl recognized Peter and accused him of being a follower of Jesus. Peter denied Jesus three times, much to his regret (Mark 14: 53-72). Only a few women, Mary the mother of Jesus, and one disciple, John, were there for him at the crucifixion. They had all scattered to the wind in fear.

It is not my intention to pass judgment on the disciples. Had I been there that night I'm sure I would have found a hole in the ground and stayed there. But I highlight the disciples' behavior to make an important point. After all that time with Jesus, experiencing his love and hearing his words about the kingdom of God, they could not stand their ground in their own strength. When things got tough, one betrayed Jesus and the others lashed out, ran in fear, abandoned and denied him. How many times have those been my responses to difficult times, even since becoming a Christian? More than I want to admit.

There is not a single expectation or demand of the Christian life that I can fulfill or accomplish in my own strength. I have tried, and it has simply lead to burn out and frustration. Going to church, reading my Bible, hanging out with other Christians are all good and important things to do. But in themselves even these activities are not enough to keep me standing when the waves crash in. I am much like the disciples at that point, lashing out, running, abandoning, and denying. Yet Jesus extends amazing love to me, even at such times, just as he did to the disciples.

After the resurrection Jesus appeared to his followers, gathering them back together. Amazingly, there is not one word in scripture that Jesus brought any of this up to them. And after forty days Jesus instructed the disciples to meet him on a mountaintop near Galilee. There he gave them instructions to make disciples of all people, baptizing them in his name (Matthew 28:18-20). He was still count-ing on them to carry out his mission of redemption to lost people everywhere. Yet even then, moments before Jesus ascended, they were confused about what was to happen. They thought that Jesus was going to Jerusalem to set himself on an earthly throne, to which Jesus said:

> It is not for you to know the times or dates the Father has set
> by his own authority. But you will receive power when the
> Holy Spirit comes upon you; and you will be my witnesses in
> Jerusalem, and in all Judea and Samaria, and to the ends of
> the earth. (Acts 1:8)

Jesus knew that the disciples could not fulfill their calling without receiving power from the Holy Spirit. Regardless of their intentions, the task ahead was simply too much for them. And so Jesus told them that the Holy Spirit would come upon them and they would be filled with his "dynamite" power. That is precisely what every caregiver, and all wounded people need in life. They need the Holy Spirit's power unleashed upon their lives. I know it was impossible for me to hold on in the journey or help another move toward freedom in my own strength. I needed help. And that help came to me through the pres-ence and power of the Holy Spirit. And this empowerment is offered to every person who asks.

The Promised Gift

I am always amazed and overwhelmed by the generosity and grace of our dear Lord. Consider what happened to the disciples. After all the mistakes they made from Gethsemane to the mountain in Galilee, Jesus tells them that they have a gift coming. That sounds preposterous, but it is exactly what the Lord said. Instead of rebuking them for their behavior or ridiculing them for their misunderstanding, Jesus tells them to wait for a promised gift:

> Do not leave Jerusalem, but wait for the gift that my Father has promised, which you have heard me speak about. For John baptized with water, but in a few days you will be baptized by the Holy Spirit (Acts 1:4 and 5).

Jesus instructs them to stay together and wait, because the Father had promised to give them a gift—the infilling of power through the Holy Spirit. They did wait for that gift, and after ten days in prayer the Holy Spirit came upon them in the upper room. He came like a violent wind, tongues of fire appeared on their heads, and they began to speak in languages they had never learned. They spilled out into the streets, and Peter, who had denied Jesus less than two months before, preached an amazing sermon about Christ, and three thousand people were saved (Acts 2: 1:-41).

This one event, the receiving of Spirit power, turned these people into bold, miracle-working disciples of the Lord. As a result of the Spirit's outpouring, they loved Jesus more than ever and became deeply committed to one another (Acts 2:42-47). They went forward to spread the gospel of Christ, perform miracles in Jesus' name, set people free from the bondage of darkness, and give their very lives as martyrs for the faith. The Holy Spirit empowered them to live and minister in ways far beyond their own abilities. And they said the gift they received is also for each of us.

Toward the end of his first sermon, Peter said, "And you will receive the gift of the Holy Spirit. The promise is for you and your children and for all who are far off—for all whom the Lord our God will call" (Acts 2: 38 and 39). 2000 years ago the Holy Spirit led Peter to say those words, because God had us in mind. No Christian is left out, for God desires that all his children walk in the fullness of the Holy Spirit's presence and power.

Jesus told the disciples that the outpouring of the Holy Spirit was a gift promised from the heavenly Father. Both words—promised and gift—are central to the infilling of the Holy Spirit in a person's life. Everyone has had someone make a promise to them. Sometimes the people are true to their word and the promise is fulfilled. Other times their words turn out to be empty. But God's promises are always true, and he fulfills them regardless of the cost to himself. The Apostle Paul said that Christ was cursed on Calvary so that we could, by faith, receive the promise of the Holy Spirit (Galatians 3:14). The promise of the Holy Spirit is linked to the very death of Jesus on the cross. Consider the great price that was paid in order for us to be empowered by the Spirit's presence.

Imagine for a moment that you had a friend who promised to take you on a month-long cruise through the Mediterranean. That would be hard to believe, given the extravagance of that type of vacation. But, you discovered that this friend went ahead and booked the best suite on the ship, purchased the tickets, established an expense account in your name for the trip, made arrangements for you to tour all the sights at his expense, and had cleared all the dates with your employer so you could go. Now with all that being done, what is the likelihood that this friend would actually come through with his promise? I would say extremely high, given his investment.

God has gone to far greater lengths so that every believer can receive the outpouring of the Holy Spirit. He had Jesus leave the wonder of heaven, set aside his glory to become a human being, experience the trials of this life, suffer a terrible death on a cross where he faced the forces of darkness, and pay for sins he never committed. All of that commitment is behind the promise God made to pour out the Spirit upon the followers of Christ. That should encourage believers to put faith in God's willingness to fulfill his words in their lives.

Many times over the years my children have used three simple words to move me to action: "Dad, you promised!" To them, my words are like money in the bank, and they feel free to draw from any promise I make. Recently our youngest daughter came home and told us that she was no longer going to live in the college dorm. She had completed her freshman year at the university and told the staff that she would not be returning to her room next year. She announced that to us, turned to me and said, "Dad, you promised that if I lived at home you would use the dorm money to buy a new car for me. When can we go looking?" How much more does our Father want his children to be confident in his word, and hear us say, "Dad you promised" and then wait in joyful expectation for the gift of the Holy Spirit.

Jesus said that the outpouring of the Holy Spirit was a gift to his followers (Acts 1:4). Being filled with the Holy Spirit is not something to be earned or given only to the deserving. It is a gift of grace received by faith. It cannot be purchased. It is freely given to those who ask. That is the "scandal" of God's entire redemptive plan. Jesus made a way, through the cross, for every Christian to receive the full benefits of the Kingdom. It is astonishing but true. Paul actually rebuked the Galatian Christians because they were teaching that the benefits of the Kingdom came only to those who were following the law. He wrote a letter in which he said:

> Did you receive the Spirit by observing the law, or by believing what you heard? Are you so foolish? After beginning with the Spirit, are you now trying to attain your goal by human effort? Have you suffered so much for nothing—if it really was for nothing? Does God give you his Spirit and work miracles among you because you obey the law, or because you believe what you heard? (Galatians 3:1-5)

Paul was adamant that the outpouring of the Holy Spirit, like all other benefits of the Kingdom, was a gift.

I write all this to encourage every caregiver and each person struggling with the effects of past traumatic wounding to ask the Lord for the infilling of the Spirit. He is the Helper who longs to fulfill the promise of God. As Christians, caregivers and hurting people already have the Holy Spirit residing within them. Being filled with the Spirit simply means asking the Spirit to unleash his "dynamite" power as he did with the disciples. Instead of facing the challenges and trials of life in their own strength, they will be able to access the strength of the Helper. That does not mean everything about the journey to healing will be easy. Not at all. But it does mean that the Spirit will bring his presence and power to bear in those difficult times. Both personally and professionally the Spirit's presence will make all the difference.

Learning from Jesus

I was a Christian for some time before I really understood the role of the Holy Spirit in the Christian life. I had a basic theological understanding, but it had not transferred from facts to an experienced reality. I spent more than a few years trying to live for Jesus in my strength, rather than allowing the Holy Spirit to empower my life. But as the difficulty of my struggle with unprocessed wounds of the past became increasingly severe, the more essential it became that I grow in understanding and open myself to a new relationship with the Spirit. When I did, asking for the promised gift, I experienced his promised infilling and it caused my Christian life to be lived at a new level. The challenges of the journey were just as intense, and as I progressed toward healing, became even more painful for a while. But the Holy Spirit brought far more to my life than I ever dreamed possible.

When Jesus told the disciples to wait for the promised gift of the Spirit, he also reminded them of what he had previously taught them about the Spirit. Once Jesus had said that streams of living water would flow from those who believe in him. The writer identified that stream as the infilling presence of the Holy Spirit (John 7:37-39). Jesus was speaking metaphorically, wanting the disciples to understand the magnitude of life the Holy Spirit brings to his followers. He does not come as a quiet butler willing to politely fill people with a teacup full of his presence when needed. Jesus was saying that the Holy Spirit would come as a living stream, bringing life and abundance to all who believe. He is not going to come simply as a gentle rain that lightly dampens the ground of their lives. The Holy Spirit wants to pour through, providing more than enough refreshment to all in need.

Toward the end of his ministry Jesus promised his followers that, upon leaving, he would send the Holy Spirit, and referred to him as the *Paraclete*. That word essentially means "one who stands along side" or "helper" (John 14:16). In some places that word is defined "comforter." Either way, Jesus is identifying the heart of the Holy Spirit's ministry. And, given the topic at hand, who does not need a helper or want a comforter? Both help and comfort are essential to dealing with deep wounds. And Jesus taught that the Divine Helper/Comforter stands ready to serve all who follow him.

Jesus also told the disciples that the Holy Spirit was the "Spirit of Truth". He said that the Spirit would teach them new things and help them know what to say when they stood before authorities (John 14:25; 15:26). Once again, what caregiver or wounded person does not need these ministries of the Spirit? There are many things a broken person does not understand, and countless times when a caregiver is not sure what to say. But the Holy Spirit stands ready to help at both points. His ministry is so critical to a believer's life, personally and professionally, that Jesus went so far as to say that it was good that he go away, because by going the Holy Spirit would come to be with them (John 16:17). His infilling is the "promised gift" that is so desperately needed by those on the journey identified in this book.

Waiting in Prayer

I remember well reading the first chapter of Acts at a time of great difficulty. And as my eyes moved across the text of chapter one, verses four and five, something stirred deep inside my heart. It seemed as if the words leaped straight from the page and into my heart. I was convinced that God wanted to pour the Holy Spirit out upon me, and that if I waited, it would happen very soon. I was practically jumping up and down inside as I read the remainder of the chapter. It told of how the disciples had waited for the Spirit by praying.

I determined that I too must wait in prayer. I also decided that I would attend a prayer meeting the next week where people who believed in the work of the Spirit gathered. For an entire week I prayed about the infilling of the Spirit, asking in faith for that out-pouring. And in faithfulness, God did grant the gift one week later at that prayer meeting. It was a profound experience that has shaped much of my life and ministry ever since.

There are several important things to consider about the way the disciples waited. The Bible says that after Jesus ascended they gathered to pray and did so for ten days before the Holy Spirit filled them (Acts 1:14). It was not an easy time for the disciples. They had experienced great emotional highs and lows over the past weeks. First they entered Jerusalem with Jesus to the sounds of praise, followed within days by his arrest, crucifixion and death. In the midst of a time of great mourning and loss they were euphoric to discover that Jesus was suddenly alive again, only to discover that he was then leaving to return to heaven.

Following the ascension, they gathered in an upper room to pray. It was obvious to them that they had not done well during the arrest and crucifixion of Jesus, and they were hiding because they feared the authorities. They were in a city under Roman occupation, where the conquering authorities had killed the Lord. And according to the final commission of Christ, they had been called by Christ to preach the gospel to the entire world. All of those feelings, realities, and expectations where present as they prayed. With all that, there is only one word that could adequately express the nature of their prayer: desperation.

The disciples did not have the luxury of mumbling a few words of prayer in ambivalence. They were in a make-or-break situation and, if anything, they were night and day crying out for God to send the "promised gift." I feel sure they took the concept of persevering prayer to a whole new level. It was not time to play at church. They needed the Helper and were desperate for his presence and power. God met them right at the point of that desperation. Ten days into the prayer meeting the Holy Spirit burst through the door, set their heads aflame, and sent then running into the streets witnessing for Jesus. They would never be the same again, and neither would the world.

What does it take then to position oneself for the outpouring of the Holy Spirit? I am not sure there really is any single key. Some people have received the infilling of the Spirit while listening to sermons, others by having someone lay hands upon them. In the case of 19th Century evangelist, D.L. Moody, it happened one day as he was walking down Wall Street in New York City. The Spirit does as He chooses and is never boxed in by a formula. Like Jesus said, "the wind blows where it wills" (John 3:8). But, having said that, I am confident that God responds when a broken person, or those called to help, cries out to Him in prayer with desperation. His heart is tender toward the broken and bruised, and He shows great compassion to those who are weak. God has promised to give to those who ask (Luke 11:13).

I encourage wounded people and caregivers to allow desperation to drive them to persevering prayer, seeking the "promised gift" of the Spirit's presence and power. The journey to freedom is far from easy. There are countless challenges along the way and the constant threat of high winds and strong waves. But Jesus has said that we can arrive on the other shore, free and transformed to be more and more like him all the time. And he offers a Divine Helper to walk with us all the way. We need but ask…and have a little faith! Mountain-moving, mustard-seed-sized faith will do.

Concluding Thoughts

There is no throw away suffering. Regardless of its nature or source, suffering is used by God to transform lives and bring people into a deeper, more intimate relationship with him. The pain that accompanies the journey for many wounded people need not be the pain that leads to death. It can, by the grace of God and through the power of the Spirit, become the pain that leads to birth—a new birth of freedom and transformation. Jesus has made a way for the broken to experience His healing touch in the memories of past traumatic events. And the Lord has provided a means of positioning wounded people for the release of pent up, unprocessed emotional upheaval.

I have chosen to share my story because I am on that journey of healing and the Lord Jesus is setting me free. I have not arrived at complete freedom…yet. But I am experiencing his transforming touch in places that long threatened to undo me. And I have seen more than a few internal storms with strong winds and crashing waves caused by traumatic events of the past, respond when Jesus entered and said, "Peace, be still." And what he does for me, he will gladly do for any who have found themselves on a journey not of their own choosing. There is a journey of his choosing that leads to rest and peace. May what has been shared in this book help position many people to encounter Jesus along that healing path.

Selected Reading

The Ministry of the Holy Spirit

Deere, Jack S. *Surprised by the Power of the Holy Spirit.* Grand Rapids: MI. Zondervan, 1993.

Graham, Billy. *The Holy Spirit: Activating God's Power in Your Life.* Dallas: Word Publishing Group, 2000.

Kraft, Charles. *Christianity with Power.* Ann Arbor: Vine Books, 1989.

Marshall, Catherine. *The Helper.* Grand Rapids, MI: Chosen Books, 2002.

Miller, Calvin. *Into the Depths of God.* Minneapolis, MN: Bethany House, 2000.

Pinnock, Clark. *Flame of Love: A Theology of the Holy Spirit.* Downers Grove, IL: InterVarsity Press, 1996.

Spiritual Formation

de Caussade, Jean Pierre. *The Sacrament of the Present Moment.* New York: Harper Collins, 1989.

Fenelon, Francois. *The Seeking Heart.* Beaumont, Texas: Seed Sowers, 1992.

Guyon, Jeanne. *Experiencing the Depths of Jesus Christ.* Beaumont, TX: Seed Sowers, 1975.

May, Gerald. *The Awakened Heart: Opening Your Heart to the Love You Need.* New York: Harper Collins, 1991.

Mulholland, Robert. *Invitation to a Journey: A Road Map for Spiritual Formation.* Downers Grove, IL: InterVarsity Press, 1992

Talbot, John Michael, and Steve Rabey. *The Lessons of Saint Francis :How to Bring Simplicity and Spirituality into Your Daily Life.* New York: Dutton, 1997.

Tozer, A.W. *The Pursuit of God.* Camp Hill, PA: Christian Publications, 1982.

Wardle, Terry. *Outrageous Love, Transforming Power: How the Holy Spirit Shapes You into the Likeness of Christ.* Abilene, TX: Leafwood, 2005.

Wardle, Terry. *The Transforming Path: A Christ-Centered Approach to Spiritual Formation.* Abilene, TX: Leafwood, 2004.

Inner Healing Prayer

Kraft, Charles. *Deep Wounds, Deep Healing.* Ann Arbor, MI: Vine Books, 1993.

Linn, Matthew, Dennis Linn, and Sheila Fabricant. *Healing the Eight Stages of Life.* Mahway, NJ: Paulist Press, 1988.

Seamands, David. *Healing of Memories.* Wheaton, IL: Victor Books, 1985.

Seamands, Stephen. *Wounds that Heal.* Downers Grove, IL: InterVarsity Press, 2003.

Wardle, Terry. *Wounded: How to Find Wholeness and Inner Healing in Christ.* Abilene, TX: Leafwood Publishers, 1994, 2005.

_____. *Healing Care, Healing Prayer.* Abilene, TX: Leafwood Publishers, 2001.

_____. *Draw Close to the Fire: Finding God in the Darkness.* Abilene, TX: Leafwood Publishers, 2004.

The Importance of Christian Community

Benner, David. *Sacred Companions: the Gift of Spiritual Friendship and Direction.* Downers Grove, IL: InterVarsity, 2002.

Bilezikian, Gilbert. *Community 101.* Grand Rapids, MI: Zondervan, 1997.

Bonhoeffer, Dietrich. *Life Together: The Classic Exploration of Faith in Community.* New York: Harper and Row, 1954.

Crabb, Larry. *The Safest Place on Earth.* Nashville, TN: Word Publishing Group, 1999.

_____. *Connecting: A Radical New Vision.* Nashville, TN: Word Publishing Group. 1997.

Spiritual Disciplines and Exercises

Foster, Richard. *Prayer: Finding the Heart's True Home.* San Francisco, CA: Harper Collins, 1992.

Foster, Richard and James Bryan Smith. *Devotional Classics: Selected Readings for Individuals and Groups.* New York: Harper Collins, 1993

Hallesby, Ole. *Prayer.* Minneapolis, MN: Augsburg Press, 1994.

Mulholland, Robert. *Shaped by the Word:* Nashville, TN: Upper Room, 1985.

Wardle, Terry. *Helping Others on the Journey: A Guide for Those Who Seek to Mentor Others to Maturity in Christ.* Kent, England: Sovereign World, 2004

Willard, Dallas. *The Spirit of the Disciplines.* New York; Harper and Row, 1988.

Trauma and Trauma Treatment

Friesen, James G. et al. *The Life Model: Living From the Heart Jesus Gave You.* Pasadena, CA: Shepherds House, 2000.

Levine, Peter A. *Waking the Tiger: Healing Trauma.* Berkley, CA. North Atlantic Books, 1997.

Rothschild, Babette. *The Body Remembers: The Psychophysiology of Trauma and Trauma Treatment.* New York: W.W. Norton, 2000.

_____. *The Body Remembers Casebook: Unifying Methods and Models in the Treatment of Trauma and PTSD.* New York: W.W. Norton, 2003.

Scaer, Robert C. *The Body Bears the Burden: Trauma, Dissociation, and Disease.* Binghamton, NY: Haworth Medical Press, 2001.

_____. *The Trauma Spectrum: Hidden Wounds and Human Resiliency.* New York: W.W. Norton and Company, 2005.

Schacter, Daniel L. *Searching for Memory: The Brain, the Mind, and the Past.* New York: Basic Books, 1996.

Schore, Allan N. *Affect Regulation and the Repair of the Self.* New York: W.W. Norton and Company, 2003.

Solomon, Marion F. and Daniel Siegel, eds. *Healing Trauma: Attachment, Mind, Body, and Brain.* New York: W.W. Norton, 2003.

van der Kolk, Bessel, Alexander McFarlane and Lars Weisaeth, eds. *Traumatic Stress: The Effects of Overwhelming Experience on Mind, Body, and Society.* New York: Guilford Press, 1996.

Notes

[1] Ronald Rolheiser, *Against an Infinite Horizon: The Finger of God in Our Everyday Lives* (New York: Crossroad Publishing, 2001), pp. 146, 147.

[2] Henri Nouwen, *The Wounded Healer* (Garden City, NY: Doubleday, 1979), p. 82.

[3] Ibid.

[4] Robert Scaer, *Traumatic Spectrum: Hidden Wounds and Human Resiliency* (New York: W.W. Norton, 2005), p. 2.

[5] Matthew Linn, David Linn, and Sheila Fabricant, *Healing the Eight Stages of Life* (New York: Paulist Press, 1988), pp. 27, 28.

[6] Bessel A. Van der Kolk, Alexander C. McFarlane, and Lars Weisath, *Traumatic Stress: The Effects of Overwhelming Experience on Mind, Body, and Society* (New York: Guilford Press, 1996), p.64.

[7] John Michael Talbot and Steve Rabey, *The Lessons of Saint Francis: How to Bring Simplicity and Spirituality into Your Daily Life* (New York, NY: Dutton, 1997), p. 63.

[8] Jean-Pierre de Caussade, *The Sacrament of the Present Moment* (New York, NY Harper Collins, 1989), p. 18.

[9] Daniel L. Schacter, *Searching for Memory: The Brain, the Mind, and the Past* (New York: Basic Books, 1996), p.17.

[10] Ibid. pp. 17, 18.

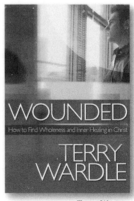